Dimensional Appliqué

Baskets, Blooms
& Baltimore Borders

A Pattern Companion to Volume II of *Baltimore Beauties and Beyond*,
Studies in Classic Baltimore Album Quilts

by Elly Sienkiewicz

C&T PUBLISHING

Illustrations by Lisa Krieshok, Berkeley, California
Electronic illustrations by Ginny Coull, Walnut Creek, California

Front Cover Photo: Original Design Album block, by J. Jane Mc. Mitchell, Dallas, Texas, 1990.
Pattern #23 Texas Treasures.
Cover designed by Julie Olson, Washington, D.C.; photographed by B. Hunt.

Editing by Louise Owens Townsend
Technical editing by Joyce E. Lytle

Design and production coordination by Judy Benjamin, P.O. Box 1887, Orinda, California 94563
Page layout by Gretchen N. Schwarzenbach

Published by C & T Publishing, P.O. Box 1456, Lafayette, California 94549

ISBN 0-914881-66-3 (Hardcover)
ISBN 0-914881-58-2 (Softcover)

Library of Congress Cataloging-in-Publication Data

Sienkiewicz, Elly.
        Dimensional appliqué : baskets, blooms, and Baltimore borders / by
Elly Sienkiewicz.
                p.   cm.
        "A pattern companion to volume II of Baltimore beauties and
beyond."
        ISBN 0-914881-66-3 (hardcover)
        ISBN 0-914881-58-2 (softcover)
        1. Appliqué—Patterns. 2. Album quilts—Maryland—Baltimore.
3. Patchwork—Patterns. 4. Decoration and ornament—Plant forms.
I. Sienkiewicz, Elly. Baltimore beauties and beyond. II. Title.
TT779.S544   1993
746.44'5—dc20   92-56192
                                                                                    CIP

Six articles that Elly Sienkiewicz wrote have, in part, been included in this book. Those articles appeared in
Quilter's Newsletter Magazine (1989 through 1991) and in the December 1992 *Threads* Magazine.

Aleene's Tacky Glue is a trademark of Aleene's Division, Artis, Inc. Decca Oil Paintstick is a registered
trademark of Decart Inc. Gem Tac is a product of Beason Chemical Company. Magic® Sizing is a
registered trademark of Dial Corporation. Perfect Pleater and ThreadFuse are registered trademarks of
Clotilde. Pigma SDK .01 pen is a registered trademark of Sakura Color Products Corporation of
America. Pilot SC-UF is a registered trademark of the Pilot Pen Corporation of America. RIT® is a
registered trademark of CPC International. Solvy, Sulky, and Sulky Solvy are registered trademarks of
Sulky of America. Stix a Lot is a registered trademark of Sewing International. Tear-Away is a brand
name of Sew Art International. Ultrasuede is a registered trademark of Springs Industries.

Printed in Hong Kong
First Edition

10   9   8   7   6   5   4   3   2

Contents

The Color Section begins after Page 80.

Acknowledgments

This book is itself an Album, a collection on a theme. Its evolution I can regard only with gratitude. So many have inspired it, contributed to it, believed in it, or simply done their job with talent, integrity, efficiency, courteousness, and old-fashioned dependability. As with those who journey together, we've become bound by friendship. To each of you, thank you. Thank you for making of this book, a Friendship Album. And to my family, I trust you know how your support has warmed my heart.

My warm gratitude to Todd and Tony Hensley, my publishers, and to Diane Pedersen, our Editorial Director. A special welcome and thank you to Louise Townsend, friend and now editor, and to Denise Scott, my skilled assistant whose efforts have been invaluable on three books now. Thank you to Lisa Krieshock and Judy Benjamin whom I'm so pleased to work with, and to Joyce Lytle and Ginny Coull who provided help and happy solutions. Thank you to the needleartists named herein who contributed time, talent, patterns, and information for this book. You made it conceivable. My appreciation, too, to Ardis and Robert James for contributing a photo from their wonderful quilt collection, and to Fairfield Processing, which has provided the batting for quilts now being quilted to complete the *Baltimore Beauties* series.

This book is dedicated to Erica Lynn Hamilton Weeder

My sister Erica: bright, talented, beautiful, organized, efficient, and responsible. My guide, my colleague, my anchor on familial seas. What hope there is for the world, when squabbling sisters can become forever friends!

BEVERLY'S BEAUTY, an original block with Ten Penny Roses by Beverly Friedline Schiavoni, 1990. No pattern given. (Photo: S. Risedorph)

Author's Preface

Lunch with friends after the show "Baltimore Album Quilts" at the Baltimore Museum of Art sounded like a welcome change from tending my "quilt shop by mail" catalog business. My interest in those particular antebellum quilts (elaborate collections of appliqué blocks) was only casual. Photos of them raised questions about textiles and techniques, which had quietly nagged me for years—years when I was much too busy to pursue answers. In fact, life as the owner of a booming small business had become tediously, unrelentingly, rather grimly full of deadlines, responsibilities, and obligations. I missed my young family, my quiltmaking, my friends. Yes, I would go to Baltimore.

The bigness, the brightness, and the timeless exuberance of those quilts enveloped me at the museum. Their effect was immediate, emotional (inexplicably they brought tears to my eyes), and compelling. I've come to think of them as "the fascinating ladies of bygone Baltimore." And that brief visit with them in 1982 has changed my life. They fascinate me still, more than ten years later.

Initially, the exceptional fabric use, the paper-cut patterns, the ornate, Victorian realism within the genre, pulled me to them. But there seemed a wealth of expression, just beneath the surface. These Albums seemed so full of "sensibilities" (the favored 19th-century word for all that feeling). I looked into "The Language of Flowers," the iconography resurrected and made famous by the Victorians in their love of symbolism, classicism, eclecticism. It fit. It seemed to explain some, at least, of the mystery in these quilts. And so my descent down into the levels of expression appliquéd skillfully within the layers, had begun. In 1983, I self-published my first book, *Spoken Without a Word, A Lexicon of Symbols, With Twenty-Four Patterns From the Classic Baltimore Album Quilts*. I didn't even try to find a publisher because the book seemed so very esoteric. It was something I simply had to do. I took a loan, ran a "for sale" ad in the *Wall Street Journal* for my mail-order business, and began to revel in the company of those quilts, their times, their makers, and, most rewarding of all, great numbers of like-minded quiltmakers both here and abroad. The transition was speedy and happy: The year 1989 saw *Baltimore Beauties and Beyond, Studies in*

Classic Album Quilt Appliqué, Volume I published by C & T Publishing. Soon, *Volume III* will follow in the fragrance of *Dimensional Appliqué* and will become the eighth book in this odyssey.

From childhood I loved needlework, history, religion, art, sentiment, writing, and people. Through the Album Quilts I can have them all. Yes, I am obsessed by these quilts. They are so rich, so diverse, so soulful, such utterly bewitching ladies! Strong, quite different styles mingle within the genre. Techniques as diverse as penwork and embroidery, and textiles as divergent as velvet and calico spin out the rich *persona* of these quilts. History's drama deepens them, appearing on both the grand and the personal scale. These are veritable windows into the souls of the women who made them. Each avenue pursued in this needle art yields a wealth of information, but always leaves questions unanswered, always more paths to turn down. Their aspects queue up as each in its turn, compels me. This book chronicles the surprisingly dimensional aspects of these quilts, their ingenious manipulations of fabric, their efforts at botanical realism, and their flights of fancy. *Volume III* will explore one-layer cut-away appliqué, *scherenschnitte* (scissors-cuttings) designs, fabulous fruit appliqué, and some stunning contemporary Baltimore-style Albums the series has inspired. The affirmation and the inspiration, for me, is that this, my obsession, is the stuff of so many others' lives as well.

Made in America during the mid-19th century, the Album Quilt style was a needlework movement that swept the Eastern seaboard. Fragments of it (possibly still as sets of gifted blocks from friends and family) scattered through the "old West" and one or two Baltimore-made Albums, even seem to have survived the long clipper ship journey to California, beloved possession of some passenger among the 90,000-odd who sailed from the Port of Baltimore on the tides of the Gold Rush. Around urban centers in the East, Albums developed distinctive regional styles. The most famous of these styles is tied to the environs of Baltimore, Maryland. All Albums are collections. The ones attached by lineage or inscription, fabric and design style, to Baltimore were unlike anything anyone had seen before. Almost entirely appliquéd, the block designs differ one from another within a given quilt. They can range from simple to predominantly complex, from one-layered appliqué to the multi-layered Baltimorean mode.

The style most closely attached to Baltimore City reflected a fresh, skilled realism in draftsmanship, embellished detail, and an ornate elegance, which both expressed and reflected the complex aesthetic of the Victorian era. These quilts teem with panoramic vitality—needle art ciphers from a thriving metropolis, an ocean-skirting link between the wide world, her nation's capitol, East Coast culture and commerce, and the Westward movement. As in a photo album, details—momentous and mundane—of Baltimorean life are portrayed. Picture blocks of national and local monumental architecture, people, animals, and local sites sprinkle these quilts, zestful and noteworthy. All is garlanded in flowers—islands of flowers float on seas of creamy white background cloth. They festoon patriotic and political references, symbolically revealing sentiments on slavery, abolition, the war with Mexico, lost heroes, temperance, communal and fraternal concerns. Amid this fragrantly petaled profusion are revolutions (in transportation—canals and railroads; in shipbuilding—from wood to steel, wind to steam; in the perceived status of negroes, women, children). But if you had to choose one dominant motif, it would be nature's bounty and her blessings: fruits, trees, leaves and stems, vines and flowers. Especially flowers. And it is the unseen beauty of old Baltimore's flowers, the lingering sweetness in the air, the alluring soul, that clearly draws so many to these quilts. Their siren song pulls us, as much as their visual and tactile and technical opulence. But first it is the flowers that intrigue us. How clever! How lifelike. How beautiful. How were they made? And we start down the garden path.

Introduction

Baskets, Blooms, and Baltimore Borders star in this book's show. Together, you and I have watched them perform for a decade or more. There seems no more appropriate introduction to these celebrities (and to this book on dimensional appliqué) than to encore those utterly Victorian floral renderings whose charisma pulled us to the Baltimore style in the first place.

The Language of the Flowers.
In the flowers of the Album Quilts, one can read their very essence. Leave aside, for a moment, the needle artistry that so intrigues us. These flowers may tell a story all their own. But since they do it through symbols, those "visible signs of invisible things," let's imagine ourselves back in time, sympathetic with the mid-19th century mode. In many ways, society was more homogeneous then, especially within a community like Baltimore. There was more public consensus than we have today, more commonly held values. It reads as a time where appreciation, community loyalty, and gratitude were lauded and disaffected self-centeredness scorned. One has no sense that anyone felt "owed" anything. The era's ideals were those same Enlightenment ideals of religious tolerance, equality, and brotherhood that had shaped the Constitution—and it was some 50 years farther along the quest for their realization. Moreover, much points to many of these quilts being made by groups of people linked by institutional, religious, fraternal, or charity commitments. The fact that these quilts reflect shared assumptions about the nature of man and the universe makes it a bit easier to hear what they are saying. Fundamental convictions colored their sense of who they were and what they believed their lives to be about. We have some sense of those tenets. With various degrees of intentionality the quiltmakers seem, through their flowers, to be affirming the following "unseen things." We'll list them, as if from a lexicon.

Flowers.
An expressive symbolic language, so much a part of Victorian culture that the meanings were immediately understood by youth and adult alike. Echoes of it are still familiar to us. We would not miss the meaning in the gift of a red rose! Widespread use of symbols dates from time immemorial, long before that most elaborate of symbols, the written word. Symbols have deepened the art of our Western Civilization for centuries. But few of us, now so widely literate, have stayed fluent in its ancient symbolic tongues. The Victorians did not invent the Language of Flowers. But they are our closest ancestors to speak it, and, to us, it's theirs.

Nature.
"The pencil of God." Observing Nature was to study (and benefit from) God's goodness. It was morally uplifting. This was the "Heyday of Natural History," when studies such as botany, ornithology, and astronomy all proved the wisdom of God's plan. "Botanizing" made one feel as virtuous then as jogging does today.

Rational Pursuits.
Morally uplifting improvement of the mind and spirit. The ideal was to reflect these in one's needle art. The Moss Rose was a hybrid introduced to the United States in the 1840s. Who can doubt that the carefully inked "moss" on the appliquéd roses reflected one's horticultural observations. With equal gusto, quiltmakers recorded the Christmas Cactus and Ornamental Peppers, recent arrivals from South America. And into their quilts as well, they stitched an era of Audubon birds.

Bouquets.
Gifts of love, expressions of thanks, approbation, offerings of the earth's beauty, offerings of gratitude. Daily, habitual, heartfelt expressions of gratitude were a way of life. "Returning the blessing," "saying Grace," "asking the blessing" over one's food was a much more uniform custom than it seems to be today, particularly in urban areas. ("For all the good gifts of this day, for food, and family, and friends, let us give thanks, our Heavenly Father," went my Grandmother's grace.)

Floral Containers.
Cornucopias, baskets, urns, ribbons tying bouquets—these were holders for Life's Blessings. This meaning is familiar to us in Thanksgiving's overflowing cornucopia. The Urn, vessel of life, speaks to us still. When we see a gravestone urn, half-covered in heavy drapes, we recognize the symbol of a life behind the veil of eternity. To the Album

Period's popular fraternal orders, the urn symbolized incense burning; its sweet scent (shown in the Albums, perhaps, by flowers) stood for the sweetness of the good soul, rising toward heaven. The Baltimore (and beyond) quilts seem full of moral and religious reminders, teachings, affirmations. Softly stitched sentiments that were sewn again and again cemented a community together. And they said it with flowers.

The Plethora of Wreath Shapes.
Every conceivable wreath shape displays floral pulchritude in the Album Quilts. This astonishing variety may symbolize plane geometry. Geometry? Geometry, an expression of mathematical perfection, was considered an expression of moral perfection, and thus of God. You'll find the letter "G" on gravestones of the 19th century for this reason. For the same reason, a pyramid adorns our one dollar bill. Its symbolism? While the three sides of the pyramid represent different approaches (as do mankind's diverse beliefs), they all arrive at one point: the "all-seeing eye of God," itself a symbol for "truth." Plane Geometry studies the path of a point on a plane. Perhaps wreaths extoll the grace of those lines traced by a point on the Album Quilt's background cloth.

Dimensional Flowers.
Flowers were the medium; dimension was the message. Geometry (comprized both of plane and solid geometry) symbolized God, or moral perfection. Solid geometry is the study of dimensional shapes in space. And surely, the Album Quilts were an ode to the third dimension! With clear intent and great cleverness, they showed dimension (and thus, also, realism) with shaded prints to show contour, with lifelike prints of flowers and leaves, and with fabric manipulated into the dimensional shapes of blossoms. The ideal in life was to "chip off one's rough edges," and to become a "perfect square," so that the Temple of Solomon, God's Temple, could be built on earth and perfect moral order would be restored. So dimension reflected perfection. And one could stitch it into one's flowers. These beliefs seem so much a part of the fiber of those Victorian quiltmakers' lives that their pursuit was probably as much motivated by pleasure as didactics: a case of doing well by doing good.

Needle Art.
A kind of moral strength. The Cult of Domesticity promised that artful, caring investment of oneself in a happy home would surely help the nation and the world.

The Rose.
This seems to be the most frequently portrayed flower in the Album Quilts. Love, a White Rose, means Eternal Love. As love, the rose is the essence of God's love for man, and the ideal of man's beneficence, one to another. Beneficence fairly beams from these quilts, symbolically through the flowers, and again through equally flowery inscriptions thereon of poetry and prose.

The Lily.
Symbolically portrayed by the Fleur-de-Lis, the Lily seems to be the second most frequently portrayed flower in the Album Quilts. As the symbol for Immortality, the lily is also the symbol of the Rebekahs, the female Odd Fellows. The emergence of this first women's order may be strongly reflected in the Albums. The Rebekah Degree itself was a symbol of the changing status of women in America.

The Rose and the Lily.
These are the most common flowers both on the Album Quilts and on mid-19th-century gravestones, appropriate in both places for their symbolism.

The Language of Flowers was such a foreign tongue to me 10 years ago. It still is, really. But I have researched a lot of the fraternal symbols, read a lot of Baltimore history, and steeped myself in Victoriana. This wee lexicon of intents for our Baltimore flowers, rings true. In an age where we want concrete answers, quick fixes, absolutes, it takes a long, long visit with those fascinating ladies of bygone Baltimore to gain a sense of the riches they have to offer. But that's part of their indefinable sweetness, too: that lingering hint of a beauty, which appeals to many senses on many levels. So as you stitch your own flowers, toy with the idea of hidden meanings, *double entendres,* philosophical statements abloom. Such expressions would seem inevitably to make one's own art more fascinating.

Part One: Getting Started

SPRING BASKET WALL QUILT (with wire-ribbon pansies) designed by
Barbara and Steve Pudiak, made by Barbara L. Pudiak, 1991, approximately
20" x 26". No pattern given. (Photo: S. Risedorph)

How To Use This Book

Dimensional Appliqué is a workbook of lessons to be done sequentially. It is also the Pattern Companion to *Baltimore Beauties and Beyond, Volume II.* As such, much basic how-to information in the series is referred to, but not repeated here. Occasionally so much more has been learned about a subject (ruching for example), that a brief review leads into the exciting new developments. When a previously taught technique is used, its source (this book, *Volume I,* or *Volume II)* is given on a pattern's Notes. You'll find it easily in a given volume's Table of Contents. *Dimensional Appliqué—Baskets, Blooms, and Baltimore Borders,* presents a wealth of block and border patterns, plus lots of individual basket and bloom templates.

Lots of great new techniques are taught in a relaxed series of 10 sequential lessons. These focus on the making of baskets, wreaths, and dimensional flowers. Appealing patterns give all that you learn a place of honor in your Album Quilt. Following *Volume I's* format, each lesson presents a full menu of new skills, which build upon the previous ones. Irrepressibly, the first lesson, "Fancy Flowers Boutique" immediately sets you elbow-deep in roses. Momentarily leaving the Album block format, it demonstrates making rolled and gathered flowers into easy boutique gifts. Do this lesson with friends and family. It's fun! Lessons 2 through 10 resume the making of quilt squares with step-by-step instructions. Many of us have enjoyed making *Volume I's* Album blocks in study circles and classes, so Appendix I gives us yet more lessons to pursue together.

Each Lesson Block is shown in the Color Section to help you select fabric. Additional squares are pictured with patterns in "Part Three: The Patterns." Color portraits of yet more luxurious Album Quilts, both antique and modern, will inspire you. Throughout this book, when a quilt is referred to by number (as Quilt #3 for example), you'll find it pictured in the Color Section. When a specific block is referred to, for example, as "Quilt #4, block E-2," the block can be located by its letter and number. The letters refer to the block position in the quilt, reading from left to right, and

the numbers refer to position from top to bottom. And, if you are wondering about the needleartists who made the contemporary blocks and quilts pictured, see "Part Four: The Quiltmakers." For additional related books, see the bibliography in *Volume III.*

GETTING STARTED

For Each Lesson Block (Beginning With Lesson 2) You Will Need:

1. A 16" square of background fabric.

2. Cloth for the appliqués with thread to match. All the baskets, even those cut of bias strips, take no more than a "fat quarter" (a rectangle, 18" x 22") of fabric, and the blooms take scraps. If you need to purchase new fabric, quarter yards will be sufficient, except for certain flower-length bias strips. For these, you may need up to a half yard. When lengths of cloth (ribbons, tapes, or bias) are needed, approximate measurements are given in the lessons. Incorporate a rich mix of fabrics. 100% cotton remains the staple, but it can be accented with rayons, polyesters, silks, satins, rick rack, etc. Depth and texture add to the compelling appeal of dimensional appliqués. Variety in weave and fiber, as well as of surface design, augment their allure.

In cottons, look for a fine, crisp hand. Needleartist Joy Nichols, a professional seamstress, notes that the fabrics used earlier in this century for dimensional blooms, were of a lighter hand than now. She suggests some of the fine poly-cotton batistes. Tie-dyes continue to imitate something of old Baltimore's rainbow prints and give a lovely "shifting light" look to our appliqués. When Jennifer Sampou, Deborah Corsini, and I recently designed the "Baltimore Beauties" line for P & B Textiles, we sought this effect. That line also includes a background cloth, which, at 78 threads per inch, echoes the quality and color of antebellum Albums. Its attributes include receptivity to ink (and to dye) for flowers and suitability for reverse appliqué. Yet another fabric to remember for fancy flowers is synthetic suede. Lightweight, washable, and needing no hemmed seam, these "leathers" are wonderful for leaves, calyxes, stamens, even the flowers themselves. They add another texture to our blocks, yet their use in hand appliqué is unobtrusive. Of course, pretest all fabrics and ribbons for washability.

MARKING AND FINISHING THE BLOCK

Basic pattern transfer and marking instructions are in *Volume I* (pages 21-25) and explain this book's Pattern Section format well. Study *Volume I* if you have not previously used patterns from the *Baltimore Beauties* series. To some degree, all of the block patterns in *Dimensional Appliqué* involve separate-unit appliqué. This requires that you either refer back to the original design (usually aided by a light box) or have marked the background cloth for placement. My preference is to keep placement marking to a minimum: Mark the background cloth just inside (¹⁄₁₆") the pattern's lines so that your markings will not show when the appliqué is finished. Wherever possible, use a single line for a stem, a center vein line (connecting an arrow at the point and a bullet dot at the base) for a leaf, and a slightly smaller circle for a ruched or rolled ribbon rose. See "Getting Started" in *Volume I* for information on finishing the block. Before we begin the lessons, let's look at the potential of ribbons and at the various flower-making modes. And then we'll define our terms for basketry and botany.

1. Ribbons:
A wealth of exquisite ribbon is available to us from the United States, France, and Japan. "Westernized" is international today as style becomes increasingly homogenized. I find the contents notation on "French Wire Ribbon" (ribbon with a fine copper or stainless steel wire within its selvage) charmingly translatable. It reads, "Rayonne et Métal." Remove the wire, or leave it in as the method dictates. My neighbors Doris Gilbert and Carol Elliot provided a wealth of information for this book. Carol worked through a 1909 ribbon flower manual. Together we decid-

ed that only certain ribbon methods were appealing for quilt-making. Our lessons present those ribbonwork techniques, each with a quilt block venue. From the initial research, I have a chest of ribbons. And since it is a veritable treasure chest, filled at substantial cost, let me share my conclusion: One should try the wire-edged ribbon. It suits the classic Baltimore style best, is easiest to work with because you can pull the wires to gather it—instantaneously, like magic! And its coloration, which first drew me to it, is that of the rainbow fabric of antebellum Baltimore. It shades from one light selvage to increasing saturation of color at the other. It even comes in what I call "Baltimore Blue," that intense, vibrant blue one can see in the photos of old quilt blocks. Furthermore, you can appliqué all sorts of shapes out of these ribbons, which range in width from ¹⁄₃" up to 6".

2. Making Dimensional Flowers:
There are almost endless ways to make dimensional flowers. Thinking in terms of the following construction categories though, will help you develop even more varieties of your own:

1. In strips, gathered and rolled

2. In discrete shapes, seamed double and turned right side out

3. In separate shapes, gathered or pleated, then sewn

4. Hemmed petal shapes, repeated and layered

5. Stuffed and quilted appliqués

6. Raw-edged shapes

7. Fused-edged shapes (two layers of cloth fused together, cut to shape)—or non-woven fabric like man-made leathers used with a raw edge.

Note: Flowers can be worked on the final background, or worked in hand for ease and placement flexibility. *Bases:* Many flowers are most easily worked on a circle base (of muslin or tear-away paper). Lisa Schiller suggests using Solvy® water-soluble stabilizer. Sometimes I work on a paper-backed heat-and-bond web. I stitch my flower through it, then remove the paper, leaving the web to heat-fuse the bloom to background fabric.

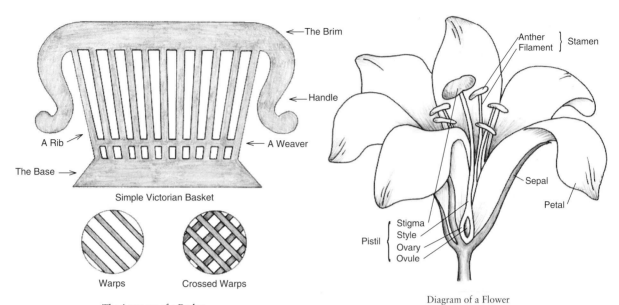

The Anatomy of a Basket

Diagram of a Flower

Where to Weave Your Baskets. You can weave your basket directly on the background cloth. This gives that classic airy look so typical of Baltimore Album Quilts. Or you can weave your baskets on a *foundation* shape (of a different cloth), which has been thread- or glue-basted to the background.

The Ribs. These run vertically and go on first. (Lesson 6 explains why it is simplest to weave a basket with an uneven number of ribs.)

The Weavers. These weave (horizontally) in and out of a basket's ribs.

The Base and the Brim. The base and the brim are often prime sites for decoration. Baltimore brims tend to end in what may have been "handles," fancy finials of astonishing variety.

Materials for Ribs and Weavers. Ribs and weavers for Album blocks can be made of many things: ribbons, finished-edge bias strips, or raw-edge bias strips.

BASKET WEAVING FOR QUILTMAKERS

The Basic Shape and Size.
Album basket shapes are wonderfully varied. The basket can run from a straight-sided basket to the ornate urn-like Victorian baskets we've seen framing the center block in Album Quilts. View the Pattern and Color Sections for simple baskets, pedestal baskets, and baskets whose bases appear to be seen from below. Some baskets have handles, others do not. Baskets can be almost any size. The basket can be heavily laden with fruits and flowers and fill only a small portion at the base of the block. Or, it can fill a third to two thirds of the design area of the block with the remaining space for its bounty. The choice is yours.

BOTANICAL BASICS FOR QUILTMAKERS

Album quilts encourage what Victorian ladies dubbed "botanizing" and then picturing your obser-

vations with your needle and thread. We, like they, are taking a fresh look at the flowers around us. Words help us conceptualize visual beauty. Here's how *Webster's New World Dictionary of the American Language* defines leaf, stem and flower parts:

Stem: any stalk or part supporting leaves, flowers, or fruit

Leaf: any of the flat, thin, expanded organs, usually green, growing from the stem or twig of a plant; it usually consists of a broad blade, a petiole, or stalk, and stipules (one of two small, leaflike parts at the base of some leafstalks)

Calyx: the outer whorl of leaves, or sepals, at the base of a flower

Bud: a small swelling or projection on a plant, from which a shoot, cluster of leaves, or a flower develops

Sepal: any of the leaf divisions of the calyx

Blossom: a flower or bloom

Corolla: the petals, or inner leaves, of a flower

Corona: the cuplike part on the inner side of the corolla of certain flowers, as the daffodil, milkweed, etc.

Stamen: a pollen-bearing organ in a flower, made of a slender stalk (filament) and a pollen sac (anther)

Pistil: the seed-bearing organ of a flower consisting of the ovary (the large hollow part of the pistul containing ovules), stigma (the tip of the pistol of a flower, receiving pollen), and style (the stalk-like part of a pistil, between the stigma and the ovary.)

Leaf Forms

This sampling of leaf forms shows some of your foliage-making options.

Leaf Kinds: Simple or Pinnate (with leaflets on each side of a common stem in a feather-like arrangement).

Leaf Margins

| Dentate (having a toothed margin) | Crenate (having a notched or scalloped edge) | Entire (having an unbroken margin, without notches or indentations) | Serrate (having saw-like notches along the edge) | Doubly Serrate | Pinnately Lobed | Palmately Lobed (having veins or lobes radiating from a common center) | Undulate |

Shapes

| Oval | Oblong | Linear | Kidney-Shaped |

| Wedge-Shaped | Awl-Shaped | Spatulate | Elliptical | Ovate | Deltoid |

Venation

| Base to Margin | Mid-rib to Margin | Parallel from Base to Tip | Pinnate | Palmate |

Part Two: The Lessons

RITA KILSTROM'S ROUND BASKET (Pattern #26), designed and made by Rita Young Kilstrom. (Photo: S. Risedorph)

Introducing The Lessons

This book runs the gamut from a lighthearted introduction to dimensional blooms (in Lesson 1: Fancy Flowers Boutique) to advanced heirloom quiltmaking. There are seven basic lessons and three advanced lessons (Lesson 6: Advanced Basketry: Artisans at Work; Lesson 9: Advanced Blooms: Filling a Vase with Fancy Flowers; and Lesson 10: Advanced Blooms: Beribboned Bouquets). Lessons 2 through 5 are basic basketry lessons with a wealth of flowers besides. Lessons 7 and 8 teach sophisticated-looking techniques through simple, easy-to-follow patterns. Encouragement to leave the lesson pattern and stitch out on your own grows stronger in the advanced lessons. The Color Section and the Pattern Section are brimful of excitement. The medallion and six border patterns presented are fertile soil for adorning with dimensional blooms as well.

More than in any of the other books in the *Baltimore Beauties* series, the blocks pictured here in *Dimensional Appliqué* are "beyond" Baltimore. The plethora of novel techniques, the very act of manipulating the cloth into bloom, and our own passion for flowers form a riptide carrying us off to uncharted waters. Perhaps dimensional flowers themselves pulled thus at the old Album style and were the catalyst that kept it so dynamic for so long. Many contemporary quiltmakers' work is featured here. Some looks very much in the classic tradition. In others, the inspiration has led overwhelmingly to innovation. It's fun to look at old Baltimore and wonder who led, who followed? And what in this book's offering may affect numbers of our end-of-the-century Albums? What's clear is that the old Album style held for a long time, over a wide area. Lots of people participated; individual innovation occurred and then became normative. We struggle with diversity in our lives, in our country, in our quilts. In America and in our Albums, we count it as our strength. It's clear that many, many of our contemporaries have learned the complex classic Album Quilt style. Now they're making it their own.

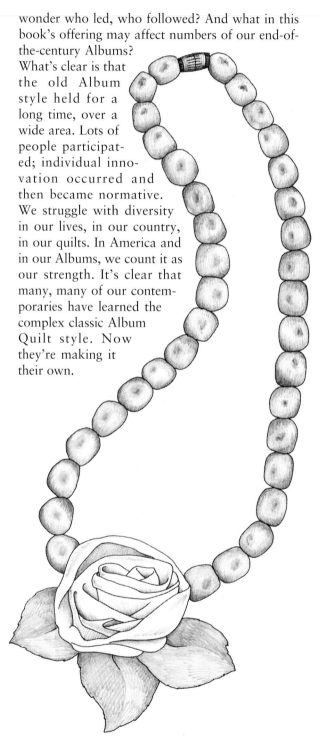

Back of Folded Rose Necklace. A pinked 1¾" Ultrasuede® circle has been glued to the back of the rose at the top and bottom only. It is raised ½" through the center to leave a tunnel through which a necklace can be threaded.

Folded Rose Necklace. Use Method #2; 18" of 1½"-wide shaded yellow-to-fuchsia wire ribbon, 1/16" center cuff, tucked raw-edged leaves.

LESSON 1

FANCY FLOWERS BOUTIQUE:
INTRODUCTION TO DIMENSIONAL FLOWERS

Gathered and Rolled Strip Flowers; Three Methods for Rolled-Wire Ribbon Roses: Method #1: (Full-Blown Rose) Using a Flat, One-Edge Gathered Strip, Method #2. (Folded Rose) Ribbon folded in half lengthwise and gathered on both selvage wires, and Method #3. (Open Rose) Ribbon folded slightly off-center from selvage to selvage and gathered along its folded length; Handsewing With Invisible Thread; Fancy Flower Leaves: Seamed and Turned, Doubled and Bonded, and Simple Tucked Leaves; Finishing as Fancy Flower Accessories and Jewelry

PATTERN:

No pattern is needed for the wire ribbon roses, nor for the Fancy Flower Jewelry and Accessories. See Color Plates #1, 2, and Back Cover.

Some things are just irresistibly pretty. Dimensional flowers certainly seem so. History repeats Baltimore's happy coincidence of motivation, talent, and materials. There, imported chintz, shaded rainbow fabrics, and textiles evoking both botanical and architectural details fueled Album blocks. Here, the ease of modern notions and expressive fabrics fan our quilts' flame. For over a decade now, the Album Quilt revival has been swelling and billowing, driven by shifting winds. Baskets, blooms, and borders, themes chosen for this book years ago, have become increasingly timely.

With the stage thus set, those taffeta-like shaded "wire ribbons" (described in "Getting Started") have only recently entered the cast. Exquisitely colored and effortlessly sculpted into fabulous flowers, they are enticing enough to make us drop everything. We want to play with them briefly, just to see a sweet bloom take shape. Thus "Fancy Flowers Boutique" makes a fine beginning lesson. We'll concentrate here on three versions of one evocative flower style, the realistic rolled-wire ribbon rose, along with its foliage. We'll stitch or glue these first efforts to small projects of our choosing. Then, having made these simple techniques our own, their blossoms will become part of our cutting garden for Album appliqué. Lesson 2 gathers them in full bloom for a ribbon basket block.

Small Brooch. Use Method #1; 18" of 1"-wide shaded pink to green wire-edged ribbon, cuffed center, yellow stamens, and tucked raw-edged leaves.

Back of Small Brooch. To finish: glue 1½" circle of Ultrasuede® to wrong side. Or substitute a "pinked" circle cut from two layers of quilt-weight cloth fused together. Glue a pin-back on the circle center.

Large Brooch. Method #1; 28" of 1½"-wide shaded pink to red wire ribbon, tucked Ultrasuede®, and tucked raw-edged leaves.

Rambling Rose. Method #1; 24" of 1½"-wide shaded lavender-to-white wire ribbon.

Hair-Comb Blossom. Use Method #2; 18" of 1½"-wide shaded yellow-to-fuchsia wire ribbon, ¹⁄₁₆" center cuff, and tucked raw-edged leaves. Whipstitch the rose to a tortoise-shell comb and stabilize stitches with glue. For 1½"-diameter earrings, use 12" of the same ribbon (cuffed its full length) for each. Add a fringed yellow center and glue the roses to earring backs. This same "earring rose" (with three small leaves) glued to a stickpin finding, makes a most elegant gift.

"Scrunchy" Ornament or Boutonniere. Use Method #3; one yard of 1½"-wide plaid ribbon (machine gathered), and tucked raw-edged grosgrain leaves.

ROLLED-WIRE RIBBON ROSES

Just working with these lusciously hued ribbons lifts one's spirits. The flowers themselves are so quick and easy to make that you could include friends and even youngsters in the fun. Relative lengths to remember are 12"-18" (small rose), 18"-24" (medium rose), and 36" for the large roses in Patterns #10 and #13. After the roses, the lesson goes on to show you three simple leaf styles used in the projects pictured in Color Plates #1 and #2. Color Plate #2 shows an assortment of findings ordered from a notions catalog. These may inspire you with useful and ornamental objects to adorn with the rolled ribbon roses you make here. Bases ("findings") for barrettes, ponytail holders, shoe clips, pins, button covers, tie clips, and earrings are all readily available from craft, variety, or specialty mail-order shops. Lovely necklaces can be made on ribbon, chain, or strung bead bases. And only your imagination limits the number of small gift items you could make: bookmarks, eyeglass cases, purses. For sophisticated wear, elegant ribbon rose stick pins or ladies' neckties look worthy of the world's finest department store offerings.

When a special friendship present is needed, consider framing a Charlotte Jane Whitehill Rose (Lesson 5) sewn to cloth inscribed with Victorian calligraphy. Faye Labanaris has fashioned just such an appealing heirloom posey in Color Plate #2. Flowers (and leaves) can best be attached to certain bases (like hair combs, barrettes, or cloth) by repeated stitching with heavy thread. On metal jewelry findings, Clotilde (proprietress of Clotilde's, Inc. sewing notions catalog) recommends Gem Tac above all other glues. For paper, or to augment the sewing on something like a hairband, Aleene's Tacky Glue™ works well. And for the easiest way to use your versatile roses, consider Stix a Lot® from Sewing International. This is a double-sided paper coated with very strong, but repeatedly reusable adhesive. Back your ribbon roses, boutonnieres, or corsages with a circle of Stix a Lot® and move them from one outfit to another. Children love the fun of this. And flower arranging on hats and jackets is a delight with this easy notion.

GATHERED AND ROLLED STRIP FLOWERS

Flowers constructed of gathered and rolled strips lend themselves to three general approaches. The main difference between the three methods for rolled ribbon roses lies in where the strip is gathered. After being gathered, the strip is rolled in the

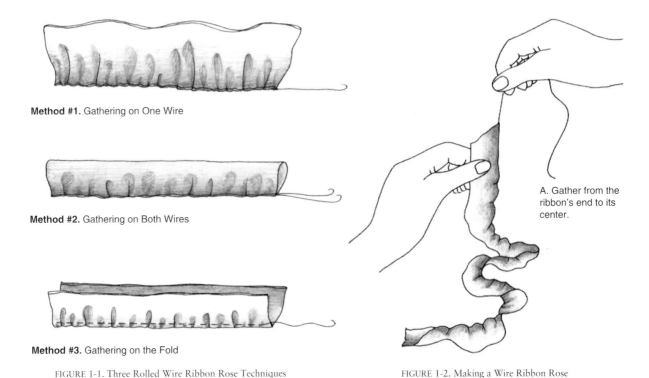

Method #1. Gathering on One Wire

Method #2. Gathering on Both Wires

Method #3. Gathering on the Fold

FIGURE 1-1. Three Rolled Wire Ribbon Rose Techniques

A. Gather from the ribbon's end to its center.

FIGURE 1-2. Making a Wire Ribbon Rose

same pattern for all three methods. We'll use wire-edged ribbon to teach these flowers because this ribbon gathers without a hitch along the wire enclosed in its selvage. With practice these blooms are thrillingly fast (shaped in under five minutes). This makes them a heady place to begin. But please note: This type of flower could also be made with a cut fabric strip that is gathered.

SUBSTITUTING OTHER FABRICS FOR RIBBONS:

If you choose to use yard goods rather than ribbon, cut the fabric on the bias, preferably, the same width as is called for in ribbon. Fabrics that can be straight-cut include high-quality polyesters, rayon jacquards, or heavy *crêpe de Chine* silks. Gathering a cloth strip can be quickened by using the longest running stitch on your machine. (Hint: With transparent 100% nylon filament in the bobbin and cotton or polyester sewing thread for the upper thread, the cloth gathers even as you stitch.) Begin by backstitching, and end with 8" thread "tails" to pull the gathering even tighter when you've finished stitching. The flower-shaping methods for gathered and rolled strip flowers are the same whether we use cut cloth or ribbon. The results differ somewhat. Experiment with types of cut-cloth flowers. Some will be endearing; others may be disappointing because that particular textile doesn't lend itself to the same floral gesture as the ribbon. If the cloth is heavier than this crisp,

fine ribbon, the greatest difference in final appearance will be caused by this discrepancy in weight and texture. You can try to imitate the ribbon's weight and taffeta-like texture in your cloth. The wire edge, too, adds distinguishing characteristics. It enables the ribbon to hold a particularly well-defined shape.

THREE METHODS FOR ROLLED-WIRE RIBBON ROSES

There are three basic approaches to making rolled-wire-edged ribbon flowers (see Figure 1-1). These roses differ in where they are gathered and in what the final flower looks like. But the manner in which the ribbon is rolled and stitched is the same for each method. The directions that follow lead you through the steps based on Method #1.

Method #1: Full-Blown Rose. (Using a flat, one-edge gathered strip)

1. Cut a 24" length of 1½"-wide yellow-shaded-to-fuchsia wire-edged ribbon.

2. Gather the rose on the fuchsia side of the ribbon's wire. (Wild or pre-hybridized roses "fade" on their outer edges, darken to the inside.) Pull to gather from each raw edge to the center (Figure 1-2A). How tightly? As tightly as it gathers, naturally, without forcing it. Bend the exposed wire back to contain the gathers at the ribbon's ends.

3. Hold the length of the ribbon in your left hand. On the righthand end, fold down a 2" tab, at a right angle. Its raw edge will hang past the gathered selvage, forming a shank or "handle" (Figure 1-2B). Use the handle to hold the rose as you make it. If righthanded, always hold the length of the strip in your left hand. Do the rolling, then the stitching, with your right hand. (From here on, all instructions will be for righthanded sewing, to be reversed by lefthanders.)

4. Begin rolling the ribbon toward its length. Start with a ⅓" fold-over at the right end and continue rolling from right to left. After rolling about an inch, fold back a ¼" cuff along the next 6" or so of the outside (yellow) edge of the ribbon (Figure1-2C). (A variation, to try next time, is to cuff the full length of the ribbon.)

5. Now hold the flower upside down. Initially, keep the selvages all at the same level, so that the back looks like the flat base of a frosting flower pulled from a cake. When you have two rounds of selvage behind the handle and you're starting the third round on the side facing you, whipstitch through the selvages and into the handle. Use a #10 or #11 milliner's needle and transparent thread.

6. Now stitch the gathered selvage to the previous round of petals, rising up on that previous petal by ⅓" as you wind around (Figure 1-2D). You'll be following a jelly-roll or pinwheel-like path. Slip your forefinger under the last round of petals so that your stitches catch just one layer.

7. When you have only about 5" of gathered ribbon left, pull the gathers back tightly on the wire once more. (They will have snuck out as you worked.) To finish, fold the tail end under towards the center of the flower (Figure 1-2E). Secure your last stitches. Cut the extended wires and handle off flush with the base of the flower.

These directions make a fine rose brooch or the perfect rose for an Album block. To sew such a glorious bloom into a quilt, you need to flatten it, as Grandma's trunk would do. Lay the rose on the

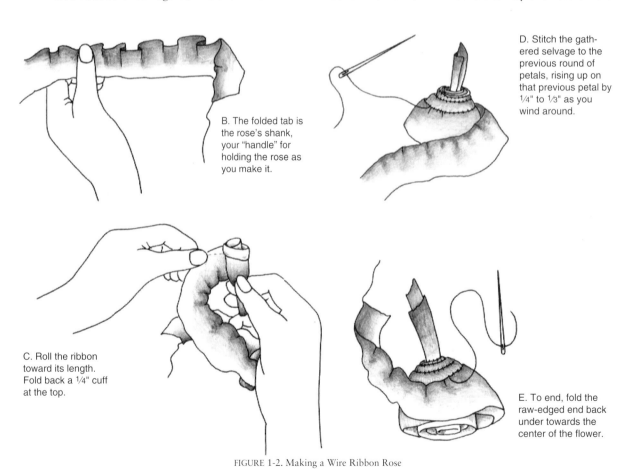

B. The folded tab is the rose's shank, your "handle" for holding the rose as you make it.

D. Stitch the gathered selvage to the previous round of petals, rising up on that previous petal by ¼" to ⅓" as you wind around.

C. Roll the ribbon toward its length. Fold back a ¼" cuff at the top.

E. To end, fold the raw-edged end back under towards the center of the flower.

FIGURE 1-2. Making a Wire Ribbon Rose

table and arrange its petals to expose the shaded ribbon's full coloration. (Push the inner petals toward its center, the outer ones forward.) With the palm of your hand, flatten the flower. This gesture gives a papery-fragile, antiquarian look. It's as lovely with Method #2 or #3 for jewelry and accessories. *Optional:* Wherever you place this rose, you might first want to insert a delicate stamen center ("Mrs. Numsen's Fringed Center"). Directions are in Lesson 2.

Method #2: Folded Rose. (Ribbon folded in half lengthwise and gathered on both selvage wires)

This is my favorite jewelry rose. It can be seen on my green stone necklace in Color Plate #2 and in my block, "Beribboned Bouquet" (Color Plate #23), featured in Lesson 10.

1. To begin the rose, pull the wires on each selvage of an 18" piece of 1½"-wide yellow-to-fuchsia shaded ribbon, and fold it in half lengthwise.

2. Fold the starting end down about 2¼" at a right angle to form the shank (the handle below the center of the rose).

3. Roll concentrically from the center out. And move the center wraps down the shank ever so slightly, winding a tight bud.

4. Wind the rose looser, with more gathers toward the outside of the bud, and keep the selvages on the same plane in the outer wraps. Roll about 5½ times, whipstitching as you go.

5. Fold the outer ribbon end underneath and secure it.

6. To finish the rose, fold the lip near the center toward the outside, pushing the center up slightly, and fold the outer lip inward, if desired. Tuck in a Mrs. Numsen's fringed center (cut from the same ribbon) and back with a set of three folded ribbon leaves.

Method #3: Open Rose. (Ribbon folded slightly off-center from selvage to selvage and gathered along its folded length)

Made out of plaid ribbon this rose (pictured on the back cover) is chic and tailored, like a boutonniere worn at the neck by a stewardess. To make a "boutonniere" type blossom, simply machine or hand gather the folded length of a 24" piece of 1½"-wide ribbon. Follow Method #1's instructions, but keep the fold on the same plane throughout the winding process. A version of Method #3 made of yellow-to-fuchsia shaded ribbon, it is sweetly floral in Lesson 10's "Beribboned Bouquet." The more detailed directions for that variation follow here. It differs from the boutonniere because it is gathered before the ribbon is folded in half lengthwise. This allows you to ease the outer petals out farther than when the gathering stitches go along two layers of the fold. Try both ways.

1. Machine or hand gather softly along the center length of 18" to 24" of 1½"-wide yellow-to-fuchsia shaded wire-edged ribbon (Figure 1-3A).

2. Fold the ribbon in half, and start rolling a tight bud center as for the folded, rolled rose, but with the folded side down, the sewn line gathered, and the fuchsia side inside. The selvages are at the outer edge of the petals. Roll firmly around the core four times, stitching back and forth through the base of the bud to hold it (Figure 1-3B).

3. Adjust the gathers so the next two rows are slightly less gathered, but take tucks to add fullness as you whipstitch them to the underneath side of the previous row. This extra fullness allows the petals to lie flat.

4. Unfold the last 6" of ribbon and pull the inner wire to gather the fuchsia edge in addition to the center gathering. To shift from folded to flat ribbon, fold the fuchsia side in toward the center and continue winding the rose and overcasting the tightly gathered fuchsia edge to the core of the flower (Figure 1-3C).

5. To end off, roll the yellow edge in towards the flower center, and secure the raw edge underneath (Figure 1-3D).

HANDSEWING WITH "INVISIBLE" NYLON THREAD

Transparent nylon thread is chameleon-like and takes on the color of the appliqué. I like to use it to sew ribbon. Use a needle threader if necessary. Use a double thread if it slips too easily out of the eye

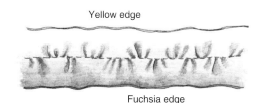

Yellow edge

Fuchsia edge

A. Gather softly along the center length of the ribbon.

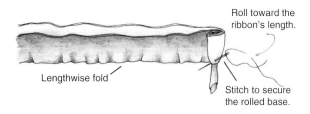

Roll toward the ribbon's length.

Lengthwise fold

Stitch to secure the rolled base.

B. Fold the ribbon in two (⅛" off-center), and start rolling a tight bud center.

C. Shift from sewing the fold to sewing the (now) tightly gathered edge to the flower's core.

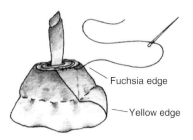

Fuchsia edge

Yellow edge

D. To end off, roll the yellow edge in toward the center, and secure the raw edge underneath.

FIGURE 1-3. The Open Rose from Lesson 10's "Beribboned Bouquet"

of the needle, and knot it with the quilter's knot. Finish your thread off with a tailor's knot finish (also called French knot finish; see page 9 in *Appliqué 12 Easy Ways!*). I use the tack stitch to sew down the basket. On the roses and leaves I use both the tack and the blind stitch. Iron your appliqué from the back, with caution; use a press cloth wet with Magic® Sizing and an iron not hot enough to melt the thread.

FANCY FLOWER LEAVES

Three-dimensional leaves work well with the fancy flowers. All of these are appropriate for use on boutique items. Some, you may incorporate in your quilt as well.

Folded Ribbon Leaves:
For a single leaf, I begin with a ½" x 3" piece of moss green damask satin ribbon:

1. Fold and tack complementary 60° angles toward the center (Figure 1-4A).

2. Repeat at each end of a 6" piece for a set of two-sided leaves (Figure 1-4B).

3. Tack the three leaves behind the rose (Figure 1-4C).

Seamed and Turned Leaves:
Seam a printed leaf right sides together with a plain backing (Figure 1-4D). Cut a bias slit in the backing and turn the leaf right side out. Top-stitch for added detail (Figure 1-4E).

Doubled and Bonded Leaves:
Fuse two scraps of green together. Trace the leaf shape on one side with the Leaf Template (Figure 1-4F). Cut the leaf out on the line. Pinking shears give the leaf a serrate edge. Try cutting some realistic printed leaves on their outline, having bonded them first to a backing.

Simple Tucked Leaves:
Left raw-edged, these are my favorites. I've made them out of quilt-weight cottons, slightly heavier threaded cottons that ravel a bit, and hand-colored polyester ribbons cut to shape.

1. Using the Leaf Template, trace a leaf on the straight of the fabric. Cut it out on the drawn line. This means that the sides of the leaf are all on the bias. Left raw, they soften slightly (like the dentate margins of a rose leaf) but go no farther.

2. Fold the leaf in half (right sides in) and stitch a tuck into it (Figure 1-4G). The leaf rounds beautifully at its base when opened. (When I am on a production roll, I simply staple in this tuck and glue the leaf to the back of the flower.) Synthetic suede, straight-cut or pinked, looks good in this leaf.

Ribbon leaves:

A.

B.

C.

Seamed and Turned Leaves:

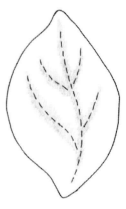

D. Seam a printed leaf, right sides together, to a plain backing.

E. Slit the back and turn right sides out. Topstitch the veins for added detail.

Doubled and Bonded Leaves or Simple Raw-Edge Leaf:

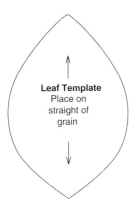

Leaf Template
Place on straight of grain

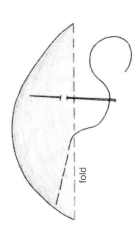

fold

F. Use this as your basic template to up- or down-size as you wish.

G. Leaf folded and tucked.

FIGURE 1-4. Fancy Flowers' Leaves

Finishing:

The leaves can be sewn or glued to the back of boutique item roses. Gem Tac glue works wonderfully. It is tough and supple on fabric, adheres well to plastic, glass, and metal. Finishing touches are important. They present the fancy flowers as objects of beauty. Back each flower with a fabric circle to clothe its mundane mechanics. Use a multi-circle template to draw the right-size circle onto your cloth. Use pinking shears to cut it out. I prefer a green backing, related in color to the leaves. Man-made suede is the most elegant. Felt or doubled and bonded cottons work, too. When the flower is nestled in greenery and backed, you can stitch or glue it to the object it will adorn. Just a few last hints wrap up our boutique lesson:

1. Remember that for a righthanded person, the pin's back needs to open on the left.

2. You will save time by buying finished accessories (headbands, barrettes) and embellishing them. The bases that you buy as crafts supplies need first to be covered before you add the flowers.

3. Many other flowers in this book's lessons are also as appealing for boutique items as for quilts. Simply work them on a circle of backing material.

4. Long-haired girls of all ages love "Scrunchies." (My daughter is pictured wearing one on the back cover.) They are so simple, you don't need directions. But here are the supplies needed for one scrunchy: a rectangle of cloth 5½" x 28"; an 8" length of ¼"-wide elastic. With a boutonniere blossom these are downright ravishing!

LESSON 2

VICTORIAN RIBBON BASKET WITH WIRE RIBBON ROSES

Basket Making on a Design Board; Non-Woven Ribbon Basketry; Double-Sided Basting Tape; Placement-Marking for Separate-Unit Appliqué; Sticky Paper Template Material; Leaves as a Design Element; Inked Leaves and Rose Moss; Mrs. Numsen's Fringed Centers; Wire Ribbon Pansies, Dahlias, and Primroses

VICTORIAN RIBBON BASKET WITH ROLLED WIRE ROSES

PATTERN:

"Victorian Ribbon Basket with Rolled Wire Roses," Pattern #13. See Color Plate 3.

Album Baskets overflowed with nature's bounty, a visible sign of the blessings bestowed upon us. As richly as do the ribbons, those Victorian imports grace this lesson's late-20th-century block. I have not recognized ribbons in any Victorian Album Quilts. Ribbons, though, notably enhanced their younger sisters, the Crazy Quilts. Readily available and with bound edges, ribbons ease us into basket making. Quick, eye-catching basketry is taught here to showcase Lesson No. 1's roses in your Album.

BLOCK PREPARATION, PATTERN TRANSFER, AND SUPPLIES

Review "Part One: Getting Started" for basic materials and marking the block. Refer to that information for all subsequent lessons as well. Special materials needed for this lesson are:

Basket-Weaving Board:
Use a design board for pinning the basket ribs and weavers into as you design the basket. Use it for flower making as well. A design board can be made of a 10" to 16" square of cardboard, cork-board, or corefoam. You can also use the cardboard sleeve from a fabric bolt or a fresh pizza box (which then can be used to carry your blocks).

Sewing Notions:
Milliner's #10 or #11 needles; silk pins; silk or transparent 100%-nylon thread; basting tape (Collin's "EZ Washaway Wonder Tape," ¼"-wide)

Ribbons:
For Basket, total of two yards of 1"-wide wine-red double-faced satin ribbon. 1. Cut five 5" lengths for the ribs; 2. Cut one 6½" and one 7½" length

for the base; 3. Cut one 24" length for the brim. Back each piece of cut ribbon (except the brim) with basting tape.

For Roses, total of four one-yard cuts of 1½"-wide shaded wire ribbon. Cut two of fuchsia-to-yellow, and cut two of rose-to-wine-red.

For Stamens/Mrs. Numsen's Fringed Centers, total of 6" length of 1½"-wide yellow-to-fuchsia ribbon (or scraps of yellow cloth).

BASKET MAKING ON A DESIGN BOARD

1. Pin the paper pattern to the design board. Iron the block fabric into quarters. Pin this cloth right side up over the pattern. Match its folds to the dotted line, which marks the pattern's center.

2. Just before placing a ribbon strip, remove the basting tape's protective backing. Lay the ribs first, overlapping the base and brim lines. When all are in place, trim the ribs back to ¼" within the base and brim lines (Figure 2-1).

3. Lay the shorter base strip down first, then the longer one. Use a bit of tape to hem the raw-edged ends of the base under before sewing.

4. *The Brim:* Lay a 5½" strip of basting tape, centered lengthwise inside the drawn brim lines. Lay the brim ribbon (also centered) across the basting tape. Give this rustic slat basket a Victorian look by folding the brim ends into a graceful handle. Pin the folds at either end of the brim length. Follow the drawn pattern (pinning into the board to play out the design) or come up with handles of your own. Slip basting tape underneath to hold the basket's shape.

Trim the ribbon ribs back to ¼" within the base and brim lines.

FIGURE 2-1

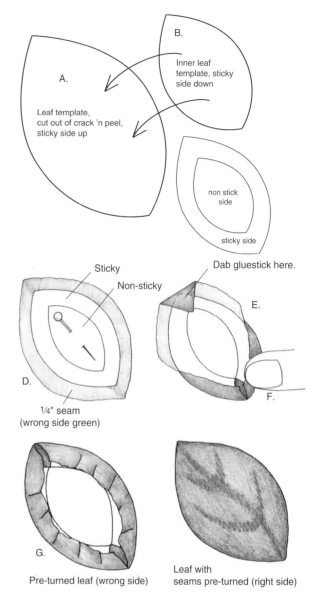

FIGURE 2-2. Pre-turning a leaf's seam, using crack 'n peel

5. Tack-stitch the basket in place. A relaxed stitch length (seven stitches per inch) is sufficient since all the edges are finished.

LEAVES

The same simple leaf shape recurs throughout this block, helping to unify and define its style. This repetition provides a low, rhythmical background melody to the jazzy, flashy roses, themselves placed in a careful pattern. Though the leaves are all the same shape and almost monochromatic, they have excitement. Intensities of color vary the green shades richly from just off white to just off black. Welcome respites of quiet, co-mingled shades come in the tie-dyes. To plan such a leaf layout, turn seams under and arrange the leaves directly on the block. Lesson 10 in *Volume I* gives numerous ways to pre-turn-under an appliqué seam. My favorite is "freezer paper inside." Yet another super-easy (no-iron) method follows.

Leaves From Crack 'n Peel:

Crack 'n peel is the colloquial name for the nametag-quality sticky paper with the peel-off protective backing. The backing is slit at intervals so that it can be "cracked" (bent open) and peeled off. Use nametags or packaged 8½" x 11" sheets from office supply stores. To make this block's leaves:

1. Cut the leaf patterns (Figure 2-2A) out of crack 'n peel label sheets. Face them with the inner leaf template (Figure 2-2B) so that only their outside edges stick (Figure 2-2C).

2. Stick the leaf to the wrong side of the green fabric. Trim the seam to ¼".

3. Remove the template, flop it over, pin it (sticky side up) to the wrong side of the cut cloth leaf shape (Figure 2-2D).

4. Miter the points: Finger-press the leaf tips back against the points (Figure 2-2E). Dab gluestick on the triangle and press the side seams to it (Figure 2-2F).

5. Finger-press the remaining side seams of the leaves to the adhesive template. The result is a "finished" looking leaf appliqué, ideal for design purposes (Figure 2-2G). Position the leaves for color, then stitch them in place. Remove the template (with tweezers) through a bias-cut slit from behind.

6. *Leaf Variation:* Shape a cotton leaf over the template, then appliqué a strip of accent-colored ribbon along one side of its center length. Because taffeta-like ribbons have a lighter hand than cotton, it makes sense to

A.

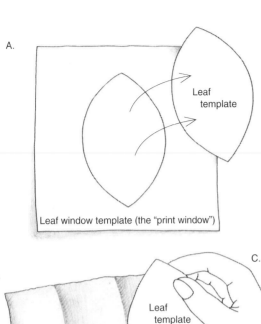

Leaf
template

Leaf window template (the "print window")

B.

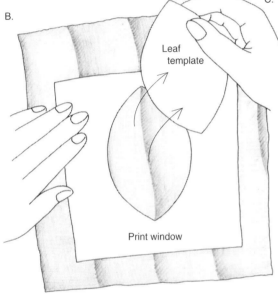

C.

Leaf
template

Print window

D.

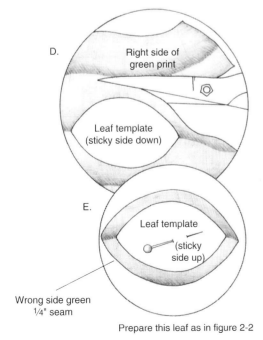

Right side of
green print

Leaf template
(sticky side down)

E.

Leaf template

(sticky
side up)

Wrong side green
¼" seam

Prepare this leaf as in figure 2-2

FIGURE 2-3. Selecting the perfect print segment by
using a print window

appliqué one on top of a full cotton leaf shape, then appliqué the two as one to the block. (Lesson 3 develops the idea of ribbon overlay appliqué in more detail.)

Print Windows:

We delight in prints. Recognizing any form of intuitive print use in a block is to share another's insight. It elates the quiltmaker in us. But how do we spot the perfect segment of a print, one that suggests realism in our appliqué? A "print window" is ideal. It helps both in the selection of a print area, and then translates that precise area into the appliqué motif. It combines the familiar ideas of a window template and that of seams-preturned appliqué.

1. On a 3" square of crack 'n peel, trace the leaf pattern. Cut out the leaf pattern carefully so that you have both a window template (the print window) and the leaf template (Figure 2-3A).

2. Peel the protective backing off the leaf template and set the template aside temporarily.

3. Hold the backed print window right side up over the printed surface, judging the effectiveness of different areas (Figure 2-3B).

4. When you find the perfect spot, hold that place with your left hand. With your right, gently stick the leaf template inside the "window," like returning a puzzle piece in a jigsaw puzzle (Figure 2-3C).

5. Remove the print window and cut a ¼" seam around the leaf template (Figure 2-3D).

6. Peel off the leaf template. Turn the appliqué shape wrong side up. Pin the leaf template (sticky side up) to the center of the cloth shape (Figure 2-3E).

7. Finger press the seam up, over, and down to the adhesive-covered template as described in Figure 2-2.

MAKING THE ROLLED RIBBON ROSES

The directions for making Rolled-Wire Ribbon Roses are in Lesson 1. Use Method #1 (Full-Blown Rose) and the full yard of ribbon per rose. Because old-fashioned roses fade toward their outside, gather the darker side of the shaded ribbon for the inner rose. Fold a ¼" cuff back nearest the rose's bud center, let it out as the whorls expand.

Toward the end of the gathered strip, space the rounds of selvage a bit more widely (⅓" to ½") to bring the rose up to the size used in this pattern. Arrange the petals, then add Mrs. Numsen's Fringed Center. To finish, pin the rose onto the block, placing it over any leaves that lie beneath it. Tack both the rose's inner and outer edges down. Use your judgment about how much to sew down. One quiltmaker advised, "Stitch enough so that it doesn't wilt in the trunk."

Mrs. Numsen's Fringed Center:
Named for its appearance in a Numsen family quilt *(Volume III),* this fringed center adds a delightful stylized realism to many flowers. It is wonderful tucked into the center of a wire ribbon rose. At first I saw it just in one antique Album, then another. One can only imagine the hothouse where such botanical hybridization was pursued. These stamens can be cut from ribbon or a variety of other fabrics. Cotton or rayon looks like corn silk; silk looks even more fragile.

1. Cut a 1½" diameter circle. Now pull the threads from the edge of the circle, leaving just ½" of solid fabric in the center (Figure 2-5A).

2. Fold the fringed circle in half, then in quarters, then in eighths (Figure 2-5B). With embroidery scissors tips, push the fringe into the center of a flower (Figure 2-5C). So simple, this may inspire blooms of your own: wedge-centered pinks bordered by folded, fringed wedges. Or perhaps round-centered asters, lacy with fringed petals.

Embellishments:
Moss roses were the darlings of the Album Quilt makers. You can stitch the rose "moss" (blanket-stitch up one side of the moss, down the other) or ink it. This is a bold and graphic block, and the slightly heavier Pilot SC-UF™ pen line suits the stylized inking for its leaves (graceful veins, dotted shadings, serrate edges) and for its jungle of moss.

A Reassuring Sleight of Hand

When we trace a shape from the right side of our pattern, which will then be used on the wrong side of the fabric, there is room for confusion. On a symmetrical shape, like our leaf, there is no problem. But because the print window is such a useful concept, you will use it repeatedly. Then you need to be confident that it works equally well with either a symmetrical or an asymmetrical pattern. To reassure folks in my classes that the print window process just described works, I do this demonstration by way of explanation:

1. Place your hand (a superbly asymmetrical pattern) palm down on the right side of your uncut square of fabric. For our purposes, the top of your hand is the traced "right side up" of the template. The palm is the sticky side, the "wrong side" of the template (Figure 2-4A).

2. Pretend that your fabric now has a cut seam allowance around this hand template. Keeping your hand right side up, slip it underneath your fabric square. Your hand's right side is to the wrong side of the fabric (Figure 2-4B). Its sticky side is waiting to have a cut seam pressed to it. When you pretend that seam is pressed to the sticky side, the fully fabric-covered side of the hand will still be right side up. Appliquéd, it and the fabric covering it, are both right side up (Figure 2-4C). So the process works

even with an asymmetrical shape. The way you trace it off your pattern works for both the print window and the template, when used to hold the pressed-under seam.

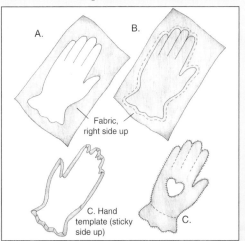

FIGURE 2-4. A Reassuring Sleight of Hand

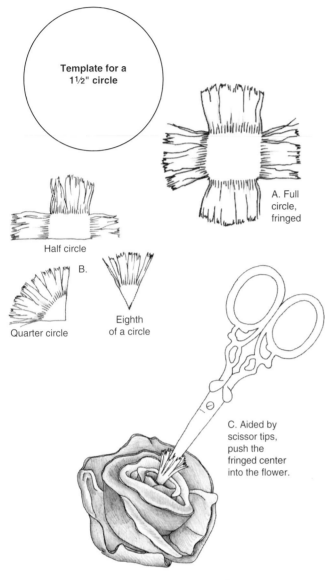

FIGURE 2-5. Mrs. Numsen's Fringed Center: Realistic Stamens for Many a Bloom!

No special preparation seems needed for this simple inkwork. The inkwork Lesson, though, in *Volume II*, is worth reviewing. Those decorative signature embellishments and calligraphed phrases contained in *Volume II*, add a delicacy of detail to a simpler block such as this one. Intricate inkwork scales them to the fine Victoriana of other blocks in our Album series. Using a press cloth, iron the ink to set it.

YET MORE WIRE RIBBON FLOWERS

While just four full-bloomed roses fill this lesson's block, you may want to fill your next ribbon basket with a variety of blooms, including the clever ones that follow. They were contributed by three talented appliqué teachers.

Wire Ribbon Pansies:

Everyone loves pansies. The Victorians loved pansies as much for their meaning as for their bold beauty. The name "pansy" theoretically comes from the French *pensées* and evokes remembrance, thoughts of—or longing for—another. In a letter, Alexander Dumas wrote, "Dear Emma, Keep these two pansies on your heart. One the colour of pain, the other the colour of love, images of our separated and united hands, one is departure, the other return" (quoted in Laura Peroni's *The Language of Flowers*). Barbara Pudiak devised an ever-so-simple pansy out of wire ribbon. While pansies are not in our lesson block, the method follows. You can design a pansy basket block, adorn a wreath with them, or tuck pansies into another block's bouquet. The method basically involves isolating a section of ruching. Once familiar with that, you can adjust the length and width of the ribbon to affect the size of the flower.

1. Use a 1¾"-wide by 6½" strip of ribbon. (1½"-wide ribbon also works with these directions.)

2. Mark five interval points, each 1½" apart (Figure 2-6A). Pencil the straight lines between the points if you like.

3. Sew in a "W" shape, connecting the interval triangles with the running stitch. At each edge point, loop the thread over the edge before you turn your stitching back to sew in the opposite direction (Figure 2-6B).

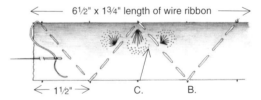

A. Mark interval points every 1½" (for a total of 5 points on either side)

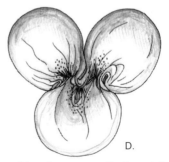

When you pull to gather, a pansy-like flower takes shape.

FIGURE 2-6. Wire Ribbon Pansy

4. *Optional Inking for "pansies, streaked with jet":* Mark the ribbon with a black Pigma SDK .01 pen, as shown (Figure 2-6C).

5. Pull the thread to gather. Three pansy-like petals form. Tuck the raw edges under the lower petal and appliqué the pansy to the block (Figure 2-6D). Try combining two of these so that four petals show at the top of the pansy. Done in narrower ribbon, these would make lovely "filler" flowers.

Lisa Schiller's Wire Ribbon Primrose
1. Cut a 12" length of 1"-wide wire ribbon. (Review *Volume I*'s ruching instructions.)

2. Ruche it into at least eight shell-like petals. Pull the inside petals tightly into a center. An outer ring of eight petals finishes the flower as in Figure 2-7A. (See "Ruching a Flower in-Hand" in Lesson 9.)

A Double-Blossomed Variation: Use 2½ to 3 feet of the 1"-wide ribbon. Ruche the whole strip. Make primrose steps #1 and 2. For the outer row, twist the ruched strip so that the lighter color is to the inside, the darker color to the outside (Figure 2-7B).

Wire Ribbon Dahlias
Both Lisa Schiller and Sue Linker generously sent me models of this charmer. They differ a bit. Lisa's directions are given first, then Sue's variations.

1. Make the center, as in steps #1 and #2 for the Wire Ribbon Primrose.

2. Cut a 16" length of the same 1"-wide ribbon into eight 2" lengths. Fold these into pointed petals: From the center, fold the right side down at a right angle, then the left (Figure 2-7C). Make eight of these pointed petals and run a thread through their bases. The adjacent selvages at the center of each petal face upward. Pull the petals into a wreath. Stitch the base corner of the first petal to the opposite corner of the last (Figure 2-7D).

3. Stitch the primrose center on top of the petal wreath so that a round ruched petal peeks out between each pointed one (Figure 2-7E).

Sue Linker's Variations: Sue adds a ninth petal to the wreath in step #3. When she stitches them

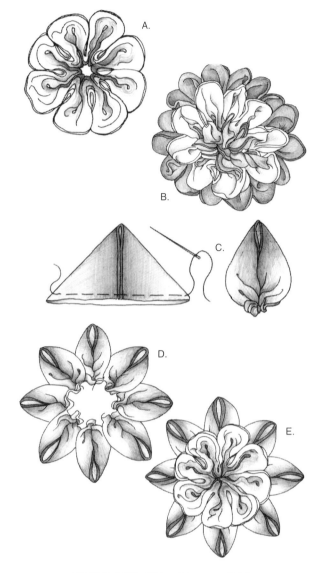

FIGURE 2-7. Wire Ribbon Primrose or Dahlia

together, she overlaps each petal base by one third. She faces the petal selvages *downward*. She suggests that one could fill the inside of the wreath with a second row of pointed petals, then a three-petal center for even more of a "dahlia look." Lisa suggests that one petal, gathered at the base, makes a winsome rosebud (Figure 2-7C, again).

An additional pattern to do using laid, non-woven ribbon work: "Kaye's Ribbon Basket," Pattern #33. Elegant-looking in hunter green, this basket is as simple as our lesson basket. The ribbon used, ¼" double-faced satin, is widely available. Easy enough for a beginner, it can use the same bouquet placement as this lesson's block. If both blocks are made, why not get variety by flopping Pattern #13's rose and foliage pattern over (trace its reverse on a light box) when you place it in Kaye's basket.

LESSON 3

FANCY RIBBON BASKETRY, *BRODERIE PERSE* BLOOMS

Building a Basket on a Cut-Out Foundation; Braided and Twisted Ribbon Basketry; Fused *Broderie Perse*; Padded Fused Appliqué; Gathered Lilacs; the Blanket and Buttonhole Stitches

PATTERN:

"Ribbonwork Basket for *Broderie Perse* Blooms," Pattern #32. See Color Plate 8.

Hand-finished, fused appliqué eases heirloom quality appliqué. First introduced in *Volume I*, this technique is expanded upon here. Capture the elegant look of heirloom *broderie perse* by blanket-stitching an appliqué's fused raw edge. *Broderie perse*, or "Persian embroidery" was an early-19th-century quilt fancywork. Motifs were cut from expensive chintz prints and appliquéd onto off-white background fabric in rather elegant arrangements. At its fanciest, not only were the appliqué's raw edges blanket stitched, but more stitchery (especially chain and stem stitches) embellished the print surface, all in the same off-white thread.

Why off-white thread? When you cut the printed blooms out, leave a 1/16" margin of the off-white background around each. The blanket stitching over that raw edge is best done in off-white thread. If the print outline were cut exactly, the threads would have to match each of its changing colors. A neutral thread matched to a neutral margin saves time and materials. The lesson was learned long, long ago.

By mid-19th century the *broderie perse* style had become simplified within the Baltimore-style. Thread (sometimes matching, sometimes contrasting) blanket-stitched the edge of prints other than chintzes, as well. Chintz motifs were often seamed under so that a non-decorative stitch (and fewer of them per inch) could be used. And the fashion of further embellishing the appliqués with surface embroidery seems to have been dropped. So there was some push, even back then, toward quicker, easier appliqué. But none has ever been so easy as it can be today. The lovely block taught here proves it.

SPECIAL SUPPLIES FOR THIS BLOCK

Sewing Notions:
Sulky® rayon machine embroidery thread, or cotton embroidery floss (single strand) and a fine

RIBBONWORK BASKET FOR *BRODERIE PERSE* BLOOMS

crewel needle for handsewing; basting tape for adhering the braided ribbon to the basket.

Double-faced Satin Ribbon:
Four yards total in two shades. Pretest all ribbon for colorfastness. Buy: one-half yard each of two contrasting 1/2"-wide ribbons for the ribs; one yard of one color and two yards of the contrasting color in 1/8"-wide ribbons for the base and brim.

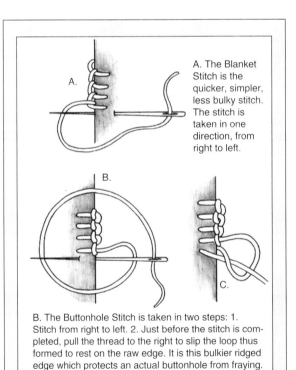

A. The Blanket Stitch is the quicker, simpler, less bulky stitch. The stitch is taken in one direction, from right to left.

B. The Buttonhole Stitch is taken in two steps: 1. Stitch from right to left. 2. Just before the stitch is completed, pull the thread to the right to slip the loop thus formed to rest on the raw edge. It is this bulkier ridged edge which protects an actual buttonhole from fraying.

The Blanket Stitch and the Buttonhole Stitch.
We tend to use the terms "Blanket Stitch" and "Buttonhole Stitch" interchangeably. Noting (correctly) that she thought I had misnamed the Blanket Stitch the Buttonhole Stitch in *Baltimore Beauties and Beyond, Volume I,* Helen Faford pointed out the difference. Here, the stitches are being worked by a righthanded person. Both stitches are looped stitches and are worked toward yourself. Notice, though, that the raw edge faces left for the Blanket Stitch, and right for the Buttonhole Stitch.

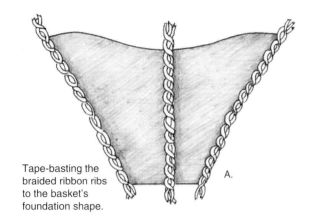

Tape-basting the braided ribbon ribs to the basket's foundation shape.

A.

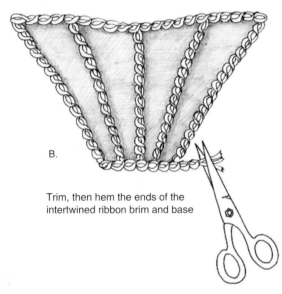

B.

Trim, then hem the ends of the intertwined ribbon brim and base

FIGURE 3-2. Braided Ribbon Basket

A. Heat-bond the outside edges only.

Leave an unfused opening here to stuff the appliqué.

B. Stuff, then heat-fuse to finish the appliqué.

FIGURE 3-3. Edge-Fused Padded Appliqué

Flowery Chintz (or other printed cotton):
Choose ⅓ to ½ yard printed on an off-white background and backed with a fusible bonding. When the appliqués have been cut out, remove the protective paper backing. Then fuse them (web side down) to the background. *Important:* Read the ironing directions on the fusible bonding's package.

MAKING THE BOUQUET

Cut out flower sprigs (leaving ¹⁄₁₆" of the background white around the edge) from your print. Make an airy, single-layered arrangement directly on the block. Keep the basic silhouette of the bouquet within a 6" radius of the center. Lay the basket's foundation shape in place before finalizing the flower arrangement. Heat-press to fuse the blooms to the background cloth. Blanket stitch the raw edges (see shaded box on page 34). Use an off-white thread matched to the background cloth and stitches ¹⁄₁₆" deep and ¹⁄₁₆" apart.

The Basket Foundation:
Cut the basket foundation out of the same chintz as the bouquet. Iron the basket base in place on the vertical fold, ¾" below the horizontal fold of your album block. Next, add the basket's ribbonwork.

Ribbonwork for the Basket:
1. Braid three one-yard strips of ⅛"-wide ribbon. Pin the raw ends to hold the beginning of the braid.

2. Every seven inches, stick in two pins, crosswise to the braid and ¼" apart from each other. Cutting between these pins, cut the braided strip into five shorter rib units.

3. Stick a strip of basting tape to the back of each braided rib. The ribs will overlap the foundation's base and brim lines.

4. Center a strip of braid over the outside edges of the basket foundation (Figure 3-2A). Place the center strip, then the two

FIGURE 3-4. Gathered Lilacs

remaining strips. Stitch the length of the outer edges of the braid down. Tack-stitch the braids' raw edges at the base and brim lines. After the braids are all sewn, trim the excess ribbon ends off to ¼" beyond those lines.

5. Intertwine just two 24" strips of ½"-wide ribbon for twined base and brim. Proceed as in Figure 3-2B. Cut the intertwined strip into a 5" piece for the base, a 13" piece for the brim. After sewing, trim the raw-edged ends off, making a ⅓" hem at the raw-edged ends. Use a tiny piece of basting tape to hold this hem under before sewing.

EDGE-FUSED PADDED APPLIQUÉ

Rita Kilstrom's block (Pattern #26) sports showy printed flowers backed with fusible bonding, but heat sealed to the background around their edges only. She learned this clever technique from a "Nancy's Notions" television show. See Figure 3-3A: 1. Seal two thirds of the appliqué's edge by ironing it to the background. 2. Stuff a small amount of polyester fiber into the opening (Figure 3-3B), then finish ironing the edge closed.

GATHERED LILACS

Rita's block includes lovely lilacs. The look of lilacs can be augmented by gathering 50¢-sized circles placed a penny apart over the cloth. Louise Allen gives clever directions for the lilacs she makes out of a small lavender print. For a substantial area, she suggests working with a larger piece of fabric, then cutting it down later to be appliquéd in the shape and size needed. Start with a 6" square to get a feel for the amounts and the method:

1. Draw repeated 1¼" circles placed a penny's distance apart onto the right side of the lavender cloth.

2. Use a running stitch around one circle's edge, then pull to gather. It will draw up into a puff. Flatten it into a shape like a square with rounded corners. Thread a needle with one strand of matching embroidery floss. Put the needle up through the center, over to the side, under, and up through the center again (Figure 3-4A). Pull the thread tightly to gather this line.

3. Repeat this stitch in a cross at the four compass points of the puff. Finish this four-lobed blossom off with a French knot center (Figure 3-4B).

An additional pattern to do using fused appliqué: "Rita Kilstrom's Round Basket," Pattern #26. This easy but eye-catching basket uses Turned-Bias Stems from Lesson 4. Her bouquet includes wire ribbon roses and print cutouts, which have been lined with flat cotton batting, interfaced, seamed, and turned right side out. Rita tacked these "quilt sandwich blooms" with French knots done in silver metallic thread.

A pattern to do combining chintz cutouts (needle-turned), ribbonwork, and Lesson 4's turned-bias stems: Carol Spalding's "Victorian Weave Basket," Pattern #25.

Yet another pattern to do using fused, blanket-stitched appliqué for the leaves and stem, is "Lovely Lane's Grapevine Wreath," Pattern #9. As you can see from the closeup photograph on the front cover of *Volume II*, this is a masterful block, best reserved for the advanced quiltmaker.

LESSON 4

THREE BASIC BASKETS

Raw-Edged Bias; Freezer Paper Ribbon Appliqué; Overlay Appliqué (both Flat and Stuffed); Turned-Bias Stems; Latticework Baskets; Speed-Stitching from-the-Back; Quarter Roses; Tucked-Circle Rosebuds; Chain Stitch and Threaded Straight-Stitch Embroidery

PATTERNS:

"Apples in the Late Afternoon," Pattern #15. See Color Plate 5. "Basket of Quarter Roses and Buds," Pattern #11. See Color Plate 4. "Ivy Basket with Bow," Pattern #16. See Color Plate 6.

Bias-cut strips, raw-edged, and braided are as relaxing to use as leaning against the very apple tree itself, savoring the sounds and smells of late summer. Hemmed bias strips take a bit more preparation, but they're incredibly versatile. Braid them; or overlay them in a diamond pattern like the Basket of Quarter Roses and Buds. Finished bias strips sculpt the fanciest woven baskets with ease. A kindred basket, capable of being plain or fancy, is the cut-away appliqué basket. Quilt #1 in *Design a Baltimore Album Quilt!* showcases numbers of these, and Irene Keating shares her charming cut-away basket in Pattern #16.

RAW-EDGED BIAS STRIPS — APPLES IN THE LATE AFTERNOON

I find raw edges in fancywork appliqué exciting. They insert an unexpected texture and charm us with their ease. In basketry, raw-edged braiding for ribs, bases, or brims imitates the roughness of wood slats, wicker, or twigs. Best of all, a bias-cut raw edge is stable: it will hold up reliably in your Album. Some pointers follow:

1. Cut raw-edged bias a scant ⅓" wide for braiding—narrower makes it too fragile. Cut a consistent width on the true bias, using a rotary cutter and grided ruler.

2. You can also mark the bias cutting line with 1/4 "-wide masking tape. Press the tape onto the bias and scissor-cut the cloth adjacent to its edges. When you remove the tape "template," it pulls the raw edges a bit, softening their margins. You can rough up the bias edges some, by rubbing your fingertips over the braid after the basket is sewn.

APPLES IN THE LATE AFTERNOON

3. For Pattern #15, cut the braiding strips ⅓" wide and 1½" longer than the drawn pattern lengths. Or, cut a longer strip of braid down to the needed size for each rib, pinning the ends to keep the cut braid from unraveling. In general, cutting the bias strips in numbers of short pieces avoids a long diagonal cut through whole cloth. It conserves yardage, while cutting it in one long strip saves time.

Constructing the Apple Basket:

Glue or thread-baste the basket foundation shape onto the block. Use basting tape to hold under the ¼" hem on the basket's brim edge. (The other raw edges will be covered by braid.) Proceed as in the previous lessons, tape-basting down the ribs first, then the two-row braid base. Tuck the raw-edged ends of the braids under the foundation. Hold them under with a bit of basting tape until stitched. Tack-stitch the braids. Catch the background fabric with some regularity to secure the basket foundation at the same time.

Freezer Paper Ribbon Appliqué:

Sometimes a ribbon is perfect—just the weight, color, and texture needed for an appliqué motif. The same 1½"-wide wire-edged rayon or polyester ribbon used for the roses in Lesson 1 sparks up the Apple block, both appearing on leaves and stripped onto selected apple halves. Cut the appliqué shape out of ribbon, using a freezer paper template inside to give it body. Alternatively, top the shape with a freezer paper template and needle-turn the seam. Be warned, though: too much heat melts the ribbon and adheres the paper so forcefully that when you remove it, the seams fray. Use a sturdy full ¼" seam and a moderate iron.

Overlay Appliqué (Flat or Stuffed):

Shaded ribbons contribute exciting color gradations and contour. Take advantage of this on apples as well as leaves:

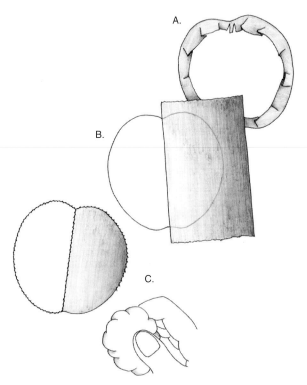

FIGURE 4-1. "Split Apples": Overlay Appliqué

1. Prepare all the leaf and apple appliqués with freezer paper (or crack 'n peel paper) templates inside (Figure 4-1A). Smoothly turn under the seams all around. Arrange these hemmed-looking leaves and apples on the background cloth. Choose the least exciting apples to jazz up with a second color.

2. For the split apples, lay a 1½"-wide strip of ribbon from the center to the right edge (Figure 4-1B). Then trim the ribbon to a ³⁄₁₆" seam at the apple's edge.

3. Appliqué the apple's ribbon-edged center first. Appliqué the left (single-layered) side of the apple and two thirds of the right (ribbon covered) side (Figure 4-1C).

4. Stuff a level tablespoon of polyester fiber under the ribbon overlay, and finish sewing the apple.

Ink Embellishment:
Ink the vein lines, serrate leaf edges, and the circular shadow of the apple's stem well (all detailed on Pattern #15). This kind of very specific characteristic (in an otherwise simplified appliqué) is Baltimore-style genius. In those old quilts, such stem wells were cut of a rimmed circle print. They accented a fruit's silhouette with a welcome insight into its beauty. Similarly, the idea of "split" fruit comes directly from the classic quilts. (Wouldn't stuffed overlay splits of shaded cloth make realistic peaches? *Volume III* will focus on fruit, both flat and dimensional. For as much creativity went into Victorian fruit motifs as into the Album flowers themselves.)

BASKET OF QUARTER ROSES AND BUDS

TURNED-BIAS BASKET OF QUARTER ROSES AND BUDS

Lesson 9 in *Volume I* reviews turned-bias strips thoroughly. We'll call turned-bias strips, generically, "stems." Completely finished, these are the easiest "stems" to weave. They are a boon to designing bouquets (both ribbon-bound and basket-held) directly on the block. For curved stems or basket weavers, cut stems on the bias.

Turned-Bias Stems:
Hints that make turned-bias stems even easier to use are shared here:

- *Using Plastic Bias Turn-Bars.* For perfect slender stems, follow these steps: A. Begin with a 2½"-wide bias strip, folded in half lengthwise. B. Into that fold, slip the narrowest width plastic turn-bar. C. Using a zipper foot, seam along the bar (fold to the right, raw edges to the left.) D. To iron the seam to the back, remove that first bar and insert the next size up. Slide the seam to the back, starch, and iron. E. Trim the seam back out of sight. The shape will be flat-edged, narrow, and very precise. (Lisa Schiller)

- Always cut the initial bias strips wider by 1½" or more than the bar width. (Excess fabric facilitates handling in the stem-making process). After turning the seam to the back and ironing the stem, trim the seam back almost to the stitch line. (Author)

- Starch the bias strips to stiffen them for easier weaving. Either spray starch or liquid starch painted on the back with a cotton swab works well. (Rene Soloman)

- Serge the bias stem seams for a nice plump "stuffed stem" look. (Salle Crittenden)

- Use a rubber office finger-protector (a finger cot) to assist twisting the seam to the back of the bias turn-bar as you iron. (Donna Hall)

- Use the narrowest basting tape underneath or masking tape on top to hold the ribs and weavers when replicating the finest woven classic basket patterns. (Mardell Pinckney)

- Cross stitch (in embroidery floss or metallic thread) effectively sews the intersections in a basket woven of narrowest stems or ⅛"-wide ribbon-floss. (Amy Cottrell)

Assembling a Latticework Basket:

A print breaks up the visual expanse of wide lattice strips. On our lesson's model, Melody Bollay used a plaid-like print reminiscent of basketry.

1. Tape-baste the first layer of the ribs (those running from upper left to lower right) to the background fabric. Trim them off on the diagonal, just inside the drawn base and brim lines. Their raw ends will be covered by the next layers.

2. Overlay the diagonal strips from upper right to lower left. The pattern shows you how the strips are layered at the basket's sides.

3. Position the basket brim and base to cover the rib ends. Hem the raw ends of both base and brim under the adjacent ribs. Stitch the basket.

Speed-Stitching from the Back:

In a recent class, I watched in amazement as Jane Smith held her block upside down and stitched her bias stems from the back. From under the block, with her left hand's fingertips, she pushed the folded edge of the stem up against the background fabric. Looking at the wrong side of the block and simply feeling the ridge of the stem, she moved along it rapidly in generously spaced running stitches. Rather long for appliqué (⅛" long and ⅛" apart) these stitches went through the background cloth and caught the underneath side of the bias stems, close to their outer edge. It held beautifully. She had matched her thread to the appliqués, but in any case it did not show, since

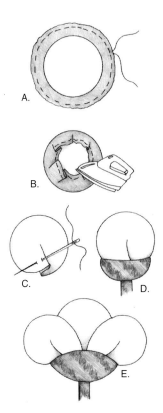

FIGURE 4-2. Quarter Rosebuds and Tucked-Circle Rosebuds

she stitched just within the shape's outline. This method takes practice and is not for everyone. It requires that the seam be held under firmly so that it will not fray. The shape must also be simple and familiar to you. And speed-stitching from the back takes a certain relaxed attitude. Loosened up to that degree, you'll find that "Easy Album Appliqué" becomes a delightful world unto itself.

Quarter Roses:

Layered-circle roses are a vintage dimensional technique. Lesson 7 teaches the classic version. For this lesson's pattern, Melody drafted a bit of perspective into her charming flowers.

1. On file cards, draw around a quarter (a 25¢ piece) to make 10 (reusable) circle petal templates. (Review Lesson 9, *Volume I:* "Perfect Grapes.") Lay the template on the wrong side of the cloth and add a ³⁄₁₆" seam allowance when you cut the circle out. Take gathering stitches about ⅛" beyond the perimeter of the template. Don't make a knot, and leave a 2" starting and finishing thread (Figure 4-2A). Tie these once so that they pull easily to gather the seam over the card like a shower cap. Dab the underneath seam with liquid starch and, leaving the template inside, iron it until the circle holds crisply (Figure 4-2B). Clip the gathering

stitches and remove the template before sewing. If, instead, you make the template of crack 'n peel, press the seam to it, and leave this template in until the partial sewing of the circle is accomplished.

2. Trace each flower pattern onto the background cloth. Draw just inside the pattern's lines to guide placement. *Note:* Sew only that portion of the petal that shows in the finished flower.

3. Stitch the outer row of petals first, then work inward. Think through the layering of the first row carefully. After sewing part way around the first petal, pull the template (if any) out with tweezers before sewing down the circle that overlaps it. When you stitch all around the flower's center, slit the back to pull the template (if any) out.

Tucked-Circle Rosebuds:
Use a quarter template for tucked-circle rosebuds: Add seam, hem, starch, iron, and remove the template. Tucked-Circle Rosebuds are simply a hemmed circle, tucked into puffed dimension by a folded dart. They can peak singly out of a calyx as in the original (Figure 4-2C). Or two can combine prettily with a flat circle center as Melody has done (Figure 4-2D).

IVY BASKET WITH BOW

CUT-AWAY BASKET DESIGN — IVY BASKET WITH BOW

This Lesson's third pattern is Irene Keating's appealing block, "Ivy Basket with Bow." Irene designed the basket by paper-folding and cutting a pattern out of freezer paper. She ironed it down to the right side of her basket fabric, traced around it with a Pigma .01 pen, then removed the template. The basket was sewn by cut-away appliqué, a technique taught in great detail in *Volume I*. This

basket is a challenge by that method because of its inward corners. The handle, and the edge binding on the basket are made from *Volume I's* superfine stem method. This particular basket would be much easier made with overlaid turned-bias stems. But it is the design potential of the cut-away basket genre that is most intriguing. Perhaps it will catch your imagination, too. Lesson 6 gives an overview of basket designing.

Chain Stitch and Threaded Straight-Stitch Embroidery:
Many of the blocks in *Dimensional Appliqué* are enhanced by the weighted line of embroidery. The thread used ranges from No. 50 machine embroidery thread (finer than regular handsewing thread) up to one or two strands of heavier embroidery floss. Color subtlety is as important in the threads as it is in the fabric. Threads with increasing intensities of hue, and hand-dyed floss are available from needlework specialty stores. As for the stitches themselves, two kinds of embroidery stitches dominate in Album Quilt appliqué: straight stitches and looped stitches. The chain stitch is one of the looped stitches. It is a tidy, controllable stitch and forms the stems and tendrils on this block. A detail of the chain stitch appears on the pattern page. On the Odense Album's Dancing Grapevine border, Quilt #17 in *Volume II*, Albertine Veenstra made wonderful tendrils by threading a green running stitch with a cocoa-colored thread. Pencil the tendril line onto the block, then follow the stitch shown here.

FIGURE 4-3. The Threaded Running Stitch

Additional patterns to do using turned-bias strips: "Folk Art Basket of Flowers," Pattern #14. This pattern is quick, classic Baltimore, and easy enough for a beginner. A turned-bias braid basket waiting to be filled is the author's "Pedestal Basket With Handle," Pattern #27.

Additional basket patterns to do using cut-away appliqué are: "Basic Basket With Braided Base and Brim," Pattern #29; "Basic Basket with Linked-Circles Base and Brim," Pattern #30; "Basic Basket With Berried Foliage Base and Brim," Pattern #31.

LESSON 5

WHOLE-CLOTH BASKETS AND SEAMED-AND-TURNED BLOOMS

Solid-Shape Baskets; The Charlotte Jane Whitehill Rose; The Many-Petaled Rose; Cannibalized Large Prints; Sue Linker's Violets, Orchard Flowers, and Daisies; Wilanna Bristow's Pleat-Bordered Basket, 1920s Roses, Gathered-Petal Flowers, Folded-Petal Flowers, and "Bell" Flowers

PATTERNS:

"Unadorned Victorian Basket of Flowers," Pattern #12. See Color Plate 13. "Regal Bird Amidst the Roses," Pattern #18. See Color Plate 28. "Wilanna's Basket Garden," Pattern #20. See Color Plate 17.

UNADORNED BASKET OF FLOWERS

Solid-Shape Baskets:

The design of even solid-shaped baskets was pushed to amazing variety in the classic Albums. When a basket is one piece, it can be printed or plain, a silhouette shape or a shape with interior cutouts. Pattern #12 is an appealing example, one we'd all be proud to have in our quilt. Though plain, its silhouette shape is interesting, distinctive,

UNADORNED VICTORIAN BASKET OF FLOWERS

and thoroughly Baltimorean. While the original has no dimensional flowers, your rendition of it could easily have some. The second block boasts a Charlotte Jane Whitehill Rose. Jeannie Austin, who made the block, has an exuberant, wonderfully recognizable style but emphasizes how much these fancy flowers are a product of regional sharing "as in old Baltimore." Flowers developed with talented fellow Washingtonian, teacher Sue Linker, are included here. The third pattern, its model wrought in bright Southwestern colors, is part of Lesson 6's "Texas Challenge." It has a pert, distinctive style and some great techniques. Wilanna Bristow, an expert on floral embellishment, designed and made the block for this series. She cites 1920s origins for many of her blooms.

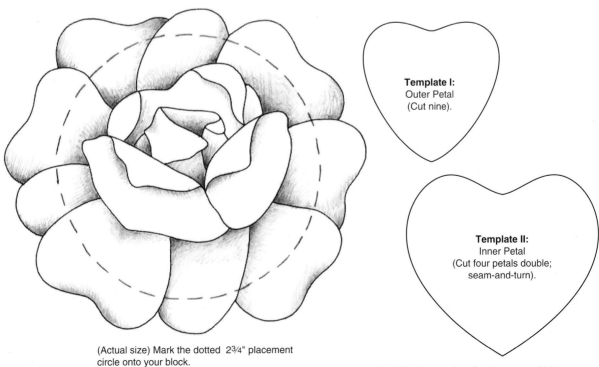

(Actual size) Mark the dotted 2¾" placement circle onto your block.

FIGURE 5-1. Version I: The original Charlotte Jane Whitehill Rose

Template I:
Outer Petal
(Cut nine).

Template II:
Inner Petal
(Cut four petals double; seam-and-turn).

FIGURE 5-2. Templates for Version I: Add ⅛" seam allowance to both templates

REGAL BIRD AMIDST THE ROSES

REGAL BIRD AMIDST THE ROSES

The Charlotte Jane Whitehill Rose:

Charlotte Jane Whitehill was a mid-20th century quiltmaker whose quilts are in the collection of the Denver Art Museum. One called "Yellow Rose Wreath" uses a beautiful layered rose. Though it is hard to trace such things, this rose stylization seems to have turned into something of a late-20th-century folk art fad. Teacher Joy Nichols introduced me to it through her "Marriage" block made for *Volume I.* Sue Linker taught me variations and shares the templates here. Faye Labanaris, teacher and member of New England's "Ladies of Baltimore North," reports that she "uses that rose everywhere." (See her roses framed, in Color Plate #2 or festively tying the vine on Quilt #7 in the Color Section.) Three versions follow Charlotte Jane's original, which rests on a base of overlapped petals. Its templates and instructions are based on its picture in the Denver Art Museum's catalog, *American Patchwork Quilts.* Figure 5-1 shows my drawing of that rose. It is sewn out of two "soft heart" shapes, Templates I and II (Figure 5-2).

The more modern Version II, The Nova Rose (Figure 5-4), is worked on a one-piece base. Yet another, Version III, The Many-Petaled Rose shown on page 45, uses many of the same templates, but again has a multi-petaled base. Add ⅛" seam allowance to each rose template. The directions that follow assume that the same fabric is used throughout each rose, although multiple fabrics could be used. (One shade can be backed with a lighter shade. This color accent shows when a reversible petal is folded back upon itself. The whole rose could darken from outer rim to the center, or vice versa.) On fabric choice, Sue Linker seeks graded sateens for her roses, and "cannibalizes" big tropical prints for the color-washed petals in her print-cut blooms. She suggests working on a

design board (cork or cardboard) to pin out the bloom first, before placing it on the quilt square where sewn leaves lie waiting.

Faye Labanaris also has a great idea for this rose: She often uses a whole printed rose as the base, then mixes print cutouts and silk hand-dyes in the petals. She carries this graphic realism to the leaves as well, using the printed outline of a leaf to guide her seamed-and-turned leaf outline. The tips

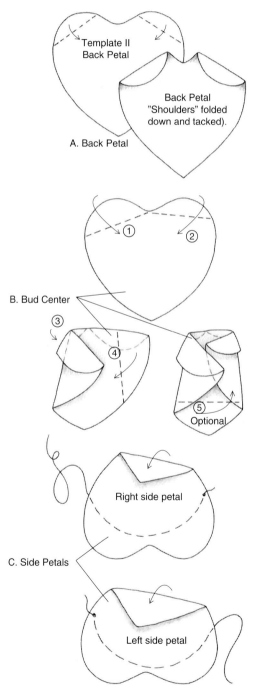

FIGURE 5-3. Constructing the Center of the Charlotte Jane Whitehill Rose

of these reversible leaves are left free to lift from the background fabric slightly; each is anchored only at its base, hidden under the shadow of the rose. Top-stitch veins for more definition, more dimensionality.

Version I: The Original Charlotte Jane Whitehill Rose:

1. Draw just inside a 2¾" circle on the background cloth itself to guide the rose's placement. (To work on a design board: Lay a 2¾" paper circle on the design board as a guide to building the rose.)

2. *Outer petals:* Cut nine Template I petals, adding ⅛" seam allowance beyond the drawn line. Arrange the petals (points to the center of the drawn circle) using the layout in Figure 5-1). Notice how some petals are tipped sideways so that just one heart "shoulder" shows. Appliqué the outer petals down.

3. *Inner petals:* Cut four Template II petals double. Seam two layered sets together, slit the back and turn the petal right side out. Finger-press the seams.

4. *Back petal:* Fold the petal tips (the heart "shoulders") in toward the center and tack in place (Figure 5-3A). Lay the back center petal in place, point to the center.

5. *Bud center:* Fold the bud center as in Figure 5-3B. Pin it in place over the back petal, point to the center.

6. *Side petals:* Fold the point of each petal down at an angle and tack in place. Fold the left petal down slightly more than the right one (Figure 5-3C). Use a gathering stitch inside the "shoulders" of the two heart-shaped side petals (Figure 5-3C, again). Pull to gather slightly. Secure the stitches.

7. Cup the right front petal (from under the left edge of the back petal) around the bud center. Mirror this with the left front petal. When the inner petal arrangement pleases you, pin, then stitch it in place.

Note: For a free-standing rose, equally as effective as an ornament or on a quilt: double-cut, then seam and turn all nine base petals as well. If your fabric seems a bit heavy, consider enlarging these templates or making the larger Version III rose, instead.

Version II: The Nova Rose:
(Figure 5-4) This rose and its templates are courtesy of Sue Linker. She promises that once this rose's basic construction is understood, "volunteer" roses aplenty will flow from your fingertips!

1. Pin the floral base to the design board.

2. Cut all the back and side petals double. Seam sets of two right sides together with ⅛" seam. Slit the back on the bias close to the bottom where it won't show, and turn the petals right side out. Finger-press the seams. Press the tips of the petals to the right side (as shown on the templates) and tack or blindstitch them down.

3. Gather the bottom of the back petal and place it on the base.

4. Fold the circle into a rosebud and center it on the back petal, raw-edged bases together.

5. The real artistry comes in cupping the softly gathered side petals around the back petal and bud to sculpt the final rose. Stitch the center in place when it is to your liking, then stitch the base to your quilt block.

6. *Optional:* For a fuller rose, cap the center with Version III's kidney-shaped front petal. When you sew this petal down you will be easing it in, cupping it with stitches taken in thread the color of the rose. All the petals are whip stitched to the base. These tiny stitches shape them further.

Version III: The Many-Petaled Rose:
(Figure 5-5) For a deeper, more lush rose, replace the single floral base with nine seamed, turned, and optionally tucked, base petals. Continue from Step 2. Sue Linker sculpts the petals more softly, spontaneously, and with more depth on this second rose. It is irresistable in hand-dyed silk or cut from a lovely oversize rose print.

To speed up the making of multiple petals:
Trace the number of petals needed (leaving a generous ½" for seams between them) onto the wrong side of one piece of fabric. Layer this, right sides together, to the underside petal fabric. Pin the center of each drawn shape, and seam the petals on the machine. Leaving a scant ⅛" seam, cut out these units, slit the back, and turn right side out.

Microwave-Dyed Cloth:
Try this on *crêpe de Chine*, silk jacquard, cotton, and ribbons. Dappled and shaded hand-dyes have

the look coveted long ago in Baltimore and once again, today. When Lorna Sattler shared fabulous hand-colored fabric, cleverly dyed in the microwave, it seemed to shine with possibilities for us all. She suggests following the basic directions on a RIT® dye package, but incorporating two specifics at the appropriate points: 1. Use glass kitchen mixing bowls and the microwave to boil the cloth. 2. When the fabric is hot and wet, lay it out and throw dry dye at it randomly. The dry dye bleeds dramatically from dark to lighter intensity, giving rich depth to the color. Boil the cloth again in clean water, repeating this process until the water stays clear. Add salt to hold color if necessary. Lorna notes that since the silk jacquard (sought for its light-catching texture) is expensive, one can perfect the technique on muslin.

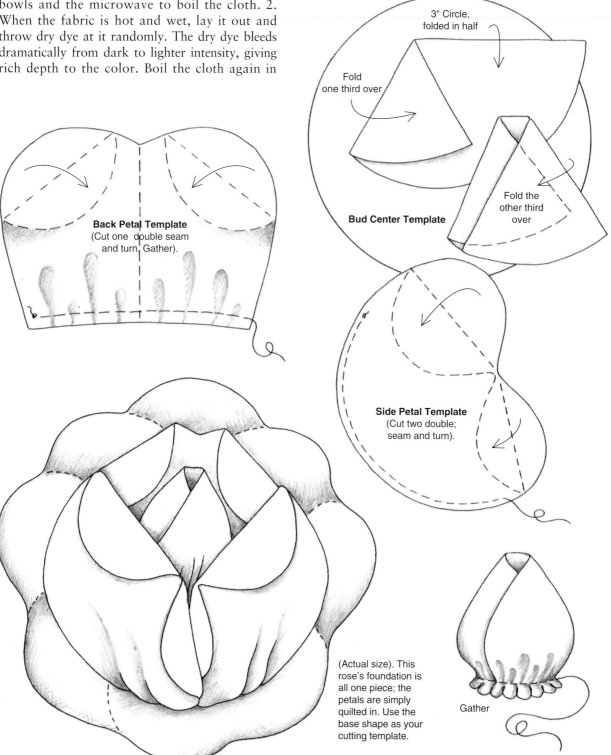

3" Circle, folded in half

Fold one third over

Bud Center Template

Fold the other third over

Back Petal Template
(Cut one double seam and turn, Gather).

Side Petal Template
(Cut two double; seam and turn).

(Actual size). This rose's foundation is all one piece; the petals are simply quilted in. Use the base shape as your cutting template.

Gather

FIGURE 5-4. Version II: The Nova Rose

Cannibalized Large Prints:

Splashy tropical prints and oversized decorator floral chintzes are available to us today. "Cannibalized" denotes rather dramatically the process of cutting these prints up solely for their coloration rather than for their realistic printed shapes. For actual templates (and window templates), Sue Linker cut flower shapes from a seed catalog. Selecting areas of larger prints with window templates and then sewing the appliqués with the cut templates, she created the watercolorist's tulips and iris in her basket wall hanging (Color Plate #27). Use the print-window technique to incorporate the cannibalized fabric concept into the Many-Petaled Rose—or any other fancy flower.

Sue Linker's Violets:

These and the orchard blossoms that come next are wonderful filler flowers. You'll see them clustered among Sue's roses in Jeannie's Blue Baltimore Basket in the Color Section. The Violet Template, Figure 5-6, is a 1¼" circle. Add the seam allowance, stitch, slit, and turn right side out. With matching sewing thread, stitch a cross over the circle (as you did in Lesson 3's lilac centers.) Pull the stitches tight to form a four-lobed violet. Stitch yellow perle cotton French knots in the center.

Orchard Blossoms:

Because of the template shape (Figure 5-7), its designer Sue Linker calls these "dog-bone flow-

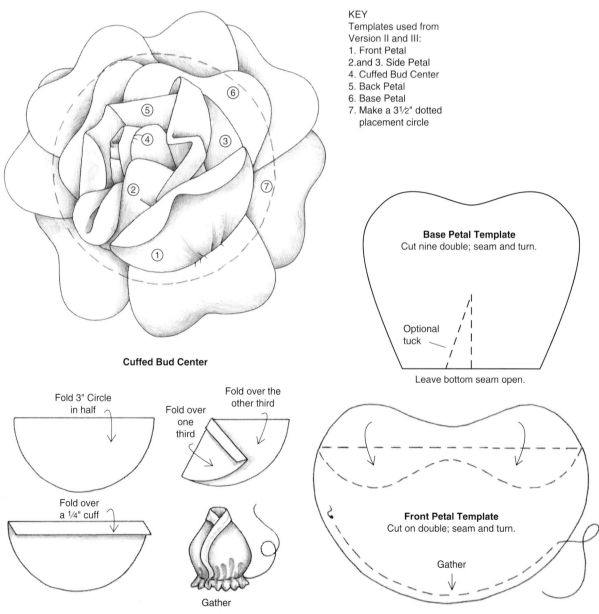

KEY
Templates used from
Version II and III:
1. Front Petal
2. and 3. Side Petal
4. Cuffed Bud Center
5. Back Petal
6. Base Petal
7. Make a 3½" dotted
   placement circle

Base Petal Template
Cut nine double; seam and turn.

Optional
tuck

Leave bottom seam open.

Cuffed Bud Center

Fold 3" Circle
in half

Fold over
one
third

Fold over the
other third

Fold over
a ¼" cuff

Gather

Front Petal Template
Cut on double; seam and turn.

Gather

FIGURE 5-5. Version III: The Many-Petaled Rose (actual size)

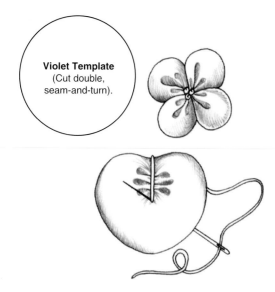

FIGURE 5-6. Sue Linker's Violets

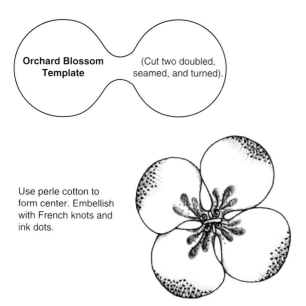

Use perle cotton to form center. Embellish with French knots and ink dots.

FIGURE 5-7. Orchard Blossoms

ers." This shape is double-cut, seamed, slit on the back, and turned. Two of these shapes are overlaid at right angles to each other. A perle cotton cross is tightly stitched through their centers to hold them. French knot stamens and ink-dotted petal throats and tips are added. Pauline Bryant designed a similar blossom. She dotted red ink onto dusty pink petals, fringed a pale yellow center, and called it a wild rose. With embroidered petal tips, even dogwood blooms are possible.

Asters or Daisies:
See Figure 5-8. Thanks to Sue Linker, these look delightfully simple!

1. Cut a rectangle of paper-backed fusible web, 2½" x 3".

2. Iron this rectangle to fabric, placing it on the bias.

3. Cut the bonded rectangle out and fuse it (again on the bias) to a second piece of fabric. When you cut it out this time, add a ¼" seam to both long edges of the rectangle.

4. Fold the rectangle in half lengthwise, and make a running stitch through the ¼" seam allowance (Figure 5-8A). Leave thread uncut.

5. With scissors (or a rotary cutter), cut the bonded side of the rectangle in parallel ⅛" strips, stopping at the seamline.

6. Pull thread to gather the petals into a circle. Sew the beginning end to the ending end (Figure 5-8B).

7. Fold the petal circle in half, and tuck it into a calyx. Or finish it off with a ½" (plus seams) circle center.

Fringed Ferns:
Ferns are the professional flower designer's favorite floral filler. Sue makes these in a fashion similar to the daisies and asters. She has made a dramatic basket thick with both ferns and roses. Use two softly mottled fern greens fused back to back for the fabric. From freezer paper, cut out varied size fern-shaped templates on the fold. To make a fern:

1. Lightly iron one template with the fold line along the fused fabric's straight of grain.

2. Carefully fold the fused fabric in half along the template's fold line. Staple the folded fabric sparsely along the fern's center vein and just outside the fern shape (Figure 5-9).

3. Cut through both layers of the fern, following the pattern. Leave ¼" at the center vein uncut. Look at pictures of different fern species for inspiration. Ferns are not symmetrical but for ease of design, I still cut mine symmetrically.

4. Running-stitch the center vein (and up into the lobes if necessary) to attach the fern to the background cloth. Sew some raw-edged ferns opened, and sew some folded for a side view.

WILANNA'S BASKET GARDEN

WILANNA'S PLEAT-BORDERED BASKET

Hem under only the sides of the solid basket foundation to Pattern #20. Big-stitch baste it to the background fabric. Then cover its raw edges with this inventive pleated base and brim:

1. Use 24" each of yellow and of goldenrod singlefold bias binding. Open them flat. (Or, cut a 1" x 24" bias strip of each color and press both long raw edges under ⅛".)

2. Pin the bias strips front to front with the top hem of each opened up. Seam along the top hem's open fold line (Figure 5-10A).

3. Fold the tape strip lengthwise, wrong sides together. The hemmed edges are now inside it. Press the strip with a bit of spray starch (Figure 5-10B).

4. Use the ½"-deep pleat on Clotilde's Perfect Pleater® (Lesson 8). Spray starch and press pleats into the length of the bias strip. This results in the basket border: facing rows of right angle triangles in yellow alternating with goldenrod (Figure 5-10C).

5. Pin the border strip to the basket base, yellow triangles to the inside of the basket. Center the strip over the raw edge of the base. Start and end with one full goldenrod triangle sticking beyond the basket's side (Figure 5-10D).

6. Because all the edges are turned under, you can sew this down with giant running stitches. Their length is on the back of the block. On the front simply tack down the folded strip at the points of the triangles as you sew

straight across the top of the border, then back across its bottom (Figure 5-10E). Cut the excess strip off, leaving a ¼" hem on the lefthand goldenrod triangle. Finish by sewing the hem under. Follow this same process on the basket's brim.

1920s Roses:

1. Per rose, cut a 2¾" x 6" strip of light rose and two to three same-size strips of dark rose.

2. Press under a ¼" hem the length of one long side (Figure 5-11A).

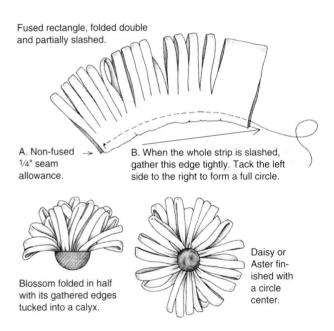

Fused rectangle, folded double and partially slashed.

A. Non-fused ¼" seam allowance.

B. When the whole strip is slashed, gather this edge tightly. Tack the left side to the right to form a full circle.

Blossom folded in half with its gathered edges tucked into a calyx.

Daisy or Aster finished with a circle center.

FIGURE 5-8. Asters or Daisies

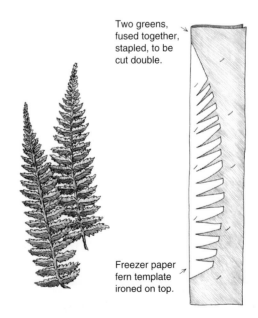

Two greens, fused together, stapled, to be cut double.

Freezer paper fern template ironed on top.

FIGURE 5-9. Fringed Ferns

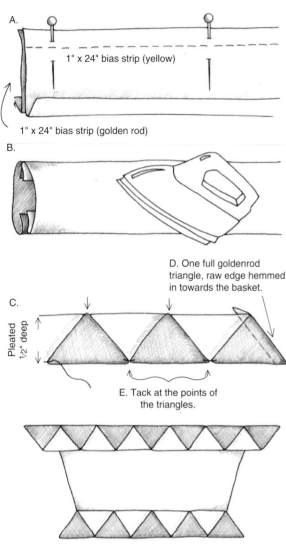

A.

1" x 24" bias strip (yellow)

1" x 24" bias strip (golden rod)

B.

D. One full goldenrod triangle, raw edge hemmed in towards the basket.

C.

Pleated ½" deep

E. Tack at the points of the triangles.

FIGURE 5-10. Wilanna's Pleat-Bordered Basket

3. Fold the hemmed strip almost in half lengthwise. The raw edge should ride up on the hemmed edge by about ¹⁄₁₆". When you sew these strips down, the raw edge will always be behind the folded edge, hidden by it (Figure 5-11B).

4. From the open edge, fold the ends of each strip up at a right angle. Finger-press, then snip off the outside triangles (Figure 5-11C).

5. With matching thread, take running stitches the length of the open edge (Figure 5-11D). Pull to gather so that the folds pile up easily upon themselves—full, but not forced. Secure the thread (Figure 5-11E).

6. *Center bud:* Fold the left end of the light rose strip to the right at a right angle. The raw edges of the strip are aligned (Figure 5-11F).

7. Pull the right end of the strip to the left so it crosses diagonally over and tucks behind the first fold (Figure 5-11F, again). These raw edges drop below the left side of the strip, opening the bud up. Tack the bud together at its base.

8. Beginning on alternating sides, cup the dark rows around the bud (Figure 5-11G), moving the seams forward in front of it (on the

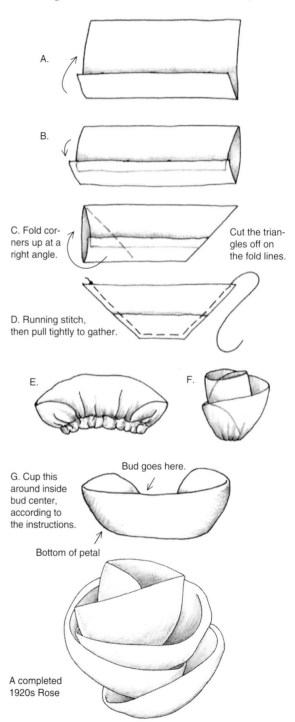

A.

B.

C. Fold corners up at a right angle.

Cut the triangles off on the fold lines.

D. Running stitch, then pull tightly to gather.

E.

F.

G. Cup this around inside bud center, according to the instructions.

Bud goes here.

Bottom of petal

A completed 1920s Rose

FIGURE 5-11. 1920s Rose

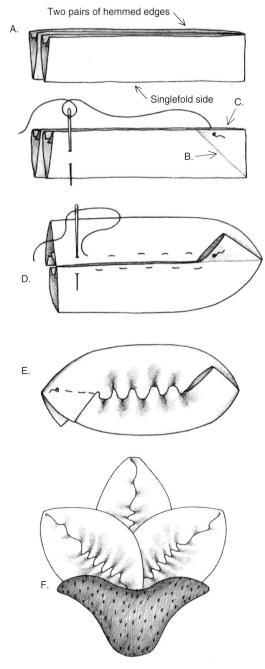

FIGURE 5-12. Gathered Petal Flowers

background cloth) so that the rose has a relaxed, full-blown look. When the flower's gesture pleases you, stitch it in place, catching the hemmed edge.

GATHERED-PETAL FLOWERS

1. Cut a bias strip 1½" x 15" for six petals (three per flower). Press a ⅛" hem in both of the long edges. From this hemmed strip cut a 2½" piece for one petal.

2. Fold the strip in half, hemmed sides in (Figure 5-12A).

3. Pinch the folded corner down at a right angle (Figure 5-12B). This forms the point of the petal.

4. Double-thread a needle in a matching color. Start the stitches ⅛" to the right of the diagonal fold (Figure 5-12C).

5. You are going to gather from that point to the lefthand raw-edged ends of the strip. But you are going to do it by taking a stitch first on one side, then the other—just like lacing a shoe. Take a stitch every ⅛" (no closer) and go through all the layers of each hemmed side (Figure 5-12D).

6. Pull the gathering thread tightly. Secure the stitches, but don't cut the thread.

7. Fold the raw edges back at a right angle and pinch to crease. Sew down the crease line (to form the second petal point) and finish off (Figure 5-12E).

8. Stitch the center petal into the open calyx, the other two overlapping in front of it (Figure 5-12F).

Folded-Petal Flowers:

1. Cut one 2½" x 3" rectangle per petal. (There are four petals in each flower.)

2. Press a 1" hem in the shorter (2½") side of the rectangle (Figure 5-13A).

3. Fold the sides in at right angles to meet in the middle (Figure 5-13B).

4. From a point ¾" down the diagonal fold, fold the right side in to the middle (Figure 5-13C).

5. Before you do the same thing to the left side, tuck its raw edge under ¼" (Figure 5-13D).

6. Fold the left side over so it covers the raw edges of the right side. Gather the bottom tightly (Figure 5-13E).

7. Tack four of these petals in a cross, and cover the raw edges with four rolls of braided rick rack (Figure 5-13F).

8. *Braided rick rack centers:* Fold 3" of medium rick rack in half lengthwise. "Braid" one strand around the other (Lesson 8). Roll the

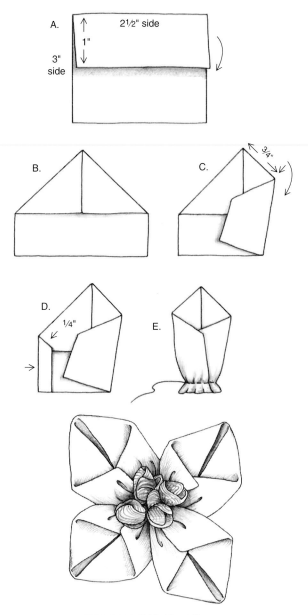

FIGURE 5-13. Folded-Petal Flowers

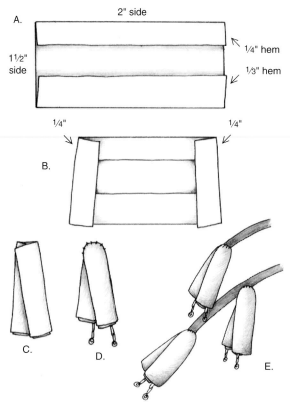

FIGURE 5-14. "Bell" Flowers

resulting 1½" braid into a bead-like oval. Stitch one over each folded petal. Place the raw edge of the rick rack on the bottom so the roll covers it.

"Bell" Flowers:

These delightful flowers are a snap to make and would look lovely in even the most classic Album block.

1. Cut one rectangle, 1½" x 2" per bell flower.

2. Press in ¼" hems on the top and a ⅓" hem on the bottom (Figure 5-14A).

3. Press in a ¼" hem on the left and right sides (Figure 5-14B).

4. Fold the right side in by ¼". Fold it in again, by another ¼" (Figure 5-14C).

5. Repeat these folds on the left side.

6. Fold the right side over the left side so that the edges are even at the top, but ¼" apart at the bottom. Pin to the background cloth.

7. Overcast the top of the righthand fold to the background. Use the stitches to pull the straight fold into a graceful, curved floral top. By this point, what you've made looks like paired bell-like blossoms (Figure 5-14D).

8. Using perle cotton, take a ½"-stitch from between the bells and end it with a French knot in the background. With the same thread take the same stitch out of the second bell (Figure 5-14E).

Other patterns to make using a solid-shape basket: "Jeannie's Iris, Pansy, and Pleated Flowers Basket," Pattern #17.

Another pattern to make using The Many-Petaled Rose: "Jeannie's Blue Baltimore Basket," Pattern #19. Sue Linker's basket wall hanging (Color Plate #27) uses this blue basket pattern filling the bouquet out with many of her flowers described in this lesson.

LESSON 6

ADVANCED ARTISAN BASKET WEAVING

The Texas Basket Challenge; Jane Mitchell's Monochromatic Basket; Basket Design Overview; Paper-Folding for Basket Shape; "Touches of Genius" Bouquet Shape; Naturalistic Appliqué; Starched Pressing

PATTERNS:

"Texas Treasures," designed and made by J. Jane Mc. Mitchell, Pattern #23. See Color Plate 14.

THE TEXAS BASKET CHALLENGE

Several years ago I was invited to teach in Texas, on the scale Texas is known for. I was impressed by the famous Texas pride in their heritage (particularly since Texas history is closely linked to Baltimore at the time of the Albums), by the warm hospitality of my Texas hostesses, and by the revivalist Baltimore-style appliqué that I saw there. Three teachers on my tour generously offered to do a block for me. I offered them a challenge: "Take a classic Baltimore block (Pattern #41 in *Baltimore Album Quilts, Historic Notes and Antique Patterns)* and do a block inspired by it." I also asked them to invite a colleague, if they wished, to accept the challenge with them. The result was that Charlotte Flesher and Wilanna Bristow of San Antonio; Roslyn Hay, Elizabeth Anne Taylor, and Jane Mitchell of Dallas; and Lisa Schiller of Houston answered the challenge. They made five breathtaking blocks, all of which are pictured in this book.

It intrigued me that I thought I could see common influences where more than one person in an area worked on these blocks. It makes sense that people who stitch and share ideas would affect each other's style as in a "folk art." In this and in so many other respects, our individual as well as group quilting (through guilds, bees, and sewing circles) seems to stitch a parallel line to quiltmakers who have come before us. It's fun, then, to imagine what sort of sharing, what sort of inspiration, what sort of challenge, led to the glorious artisan basketry so evident in the antebellum Album Quilts!

Woven baskets capture our imagination. Their possibilities are myriad. The Pattern Section contains numbers of basket shapes and Figure 6-3 illustrates some options with a Lexicon of tradi-

TEXAS TREASURES

tional basket-weaving patterns. Our lessons hitherto have eased us into much about basketry, but not woven baskets themselves. Jane Mitchell's restrained basket style is so striking filled with her Texas flowers that it is this book's cover block. It is the simplest of the woven challenge baskets and a good place for us to start. Then we'll go on to basket-making options so that you yourself can take up the basket artisan challenge!

Jane Mitchell's Monochromatic Basket:
This basket uses three closely related wine-red fabrics: #1 (a solid) for the foundation, #2 (a basket-weave print) for the ribs, brim and base, and #3 (black dots on wine) for the weavers.

1. Using Pattern #23, cut the basket's brim and base out of fabric #2. Add a $3/16$" seam allowance around the template shapes.

2. Cut a foundation shape out of fabric #1. Cut the shape $1/16$" smaller all-around than the finished basket shape in the pattern. You'll be covering these raw edges. Big-stitch baste, tape-baste, or glue-stick this basket foundation to the background cloth. Lay the quilt square over the design board so that you can pin into it as you weave.

3. Altogether you need about 65" of stems ($1/4$"-wide) from fabric #2 to make: 11 ribs, each $5½$" long. *Note:* Aim, in your basketry, for an uneven number of ribs. With an uneven number, the raw-edged ends of the weavers can always terminate under the ribs, which bind the basket's sides. With an even number this works on one side of the basket, but you need another solution on the other side. As you can see from the Color Section pictures, there are lots of other solutions—an uneven number simply starts you off problem-free.

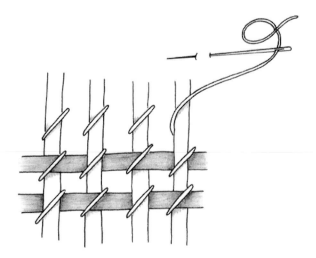

FIGURE 6-1. Tailor Tack Basting

4. You need approximately 42" of ³⁄₁₆"-wide stems made from fabric #3. Cut this into eight weavers, increasing their length as you weave from bottom to top.

5. Place the ribs first, then the weavers. Note that the space between the weavers also widens towards the brim. *Procedure:* Pin the ribs at their tops and at their bases, then weave the ribs. When the shape satisfies you, pin into each intersection. Lift this "net" from the edges, and back enough of it with basting tape to hold it for sewing. Or simply repeat history—and baste it all out carefully! *Basting Options:* Margaret Foley suggests tailor-tacking the ribs to allow you to thread the weavers through them. A tailor-tack is a well-spaced diagonal basting stitch shown in Figure 6-1.

6. Trim the ribs and weavers to the edge of the foundation shape. Then appliqué first the side ribs, then the base, then the brim. But leave the mouth of the brim open for tucking in leaves, stems, and flora. *Sewing Options:* Sewing all the exposed edges of the ribs and weavers gives your basket a tight, fine-scale look. It is necessary on an intricately woven shape like Lisa Schiller's (Color plate #12). However, on a simpler shape, like this one, you can appliqué all the ribs, but not the weavers, for example.

BASKET-DESIGN OVERVIEW

Baskets can vary in size or shape, and in the way the sides, the brim, the handle, and the base are constructed. If woven, a basket's weave pattern allows for great variety. And, as we have seen, the materials used to weave a basket are many. A basket can be built on the background fabric. Or, a basket can be built on a foundation fabric as "Texas Treasures" was. The simplest basket is one made from a silhouette cut-out shape. Each part of a woven basket is an opportunity for your innovations.

Size:

If you are designing your own basket, decide how deep it will be: roughly ¼, ⅓, ½, or more, of the block. These distinctions in basketry only fuel the collecting passion! One wants a tall basket, a small basket, a native American basket, an egg basket, a round basket, a ribbon basket, etc.

Shape:

The shapes of baskets are limited only by the imagination. Consider the figurative baskets (ducks, frogs) coming out of mainland China to entice us. Even the more traditional basket shapes are multitudinous. For us, basket shapes are easy to design. Take a minute and try one.

Paperfolding for Basket Shape:

1. Fold a standard (8½" x 11") sheet of lined paper in half lengthwise. Lined (or graphed) paper is convenient for cutting a basket whose brim parallels its base. On the fold, mark the depth you want the basket to be.

2. Pencil sketch the basket shape within the size you've bracketed. Don't labor over this. Many of us cut paper shapes better than we draw them (Figure 6-2A). Cut out your shape and see how well you've done. If you think an improvement can be made, use this first draft pattern as the basis for your next cutting.

3. Once you have a shape that pleases you, or are close to one, do your cutting out of freezer paper. Cut a freezer paper template of your final basket shape (Figure 6-2B). If you find you're cutting beautiful baskets easily, keep on for a while, and store the extra templates for later use.

"TOUCHES OF GENIUS" SHARED BY THE CHALLENGE NEEDLEARTISTS

"The a-ha! feeling," someone called it. We've all had that breath-catching surprise when a special needlework touch evokes realism or echoes a beautiful natural detail, which we recognize, but had not focused on. It happens when a stitched

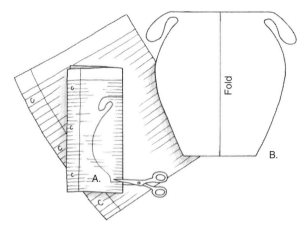

FIGURE 6-2. Paper-Cutting for Basket Design

approach is so vital that we wish we'd thought of it ourselves. The challenge blocks are full of these moments, these touches of genius. Since this is an advanced lesson, no step-by step instruction is given for the flora. The Pattern Notes point out many specifics. Some helpful approaches to advanced basketry and the flowers follow. That these have been singled out was determined by our needs in this lesson. Were I able so to extoll the individual virtues of each needleartists' work in this series, I surely would!

Bouquet Shape:
The average bouquet (whether hand or basket-held) should stay within a 6" radius of the block's center. This fits the standard 12½" square design image size conformed to in all the books of the *Baltimore Beauties* series. That same size of design image looks beautiful with a little more white space around it on a 14"-16" block. Or, you can place this same design area on a 16" block and turn it "on point" if you want to create a diagonally set quilt such as the Basket Album, Quilt #4 in the Color Section.

"Naturalistic" Appliqué:
Roslyn Hay is a native Australian who lived for many years in the Dallas area. At Sharon's Quilting Depot in McKinney, Texas, on the outskirts of Dallas, Roslyn taught many needlewomen her unique revivalist Baltimore-style techniques. A fine draftswoman, she designed an exquisite Album Quilt featuring North American wild flowers garlanding landmarks of Texas history. But the blooms she drew for her challenge block were blossoms from home. See Color Plate 11. She approached this block's flowers by tracing and drawing their shapes from both botanical drawings and photographs. Her style could be described as realistically drafted flora, painted in cloth. The

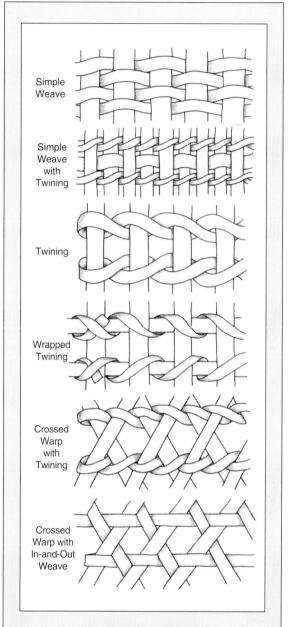

Artisan Basket-Weaving Patterns.
Once you have the shape that appeals to you, consider the weaving pattern. It can be simple: Ouide Glick designed a lovely pattern with only two ribs and no weavers. But she intertwined the two ribs at the basket's center, and interwove two stems in a pie-lattice fashion along the base and brim. If you want to get fancier, some traditional basket weaving patterns are illustrated here. Consider these once you've settled on the vessel's size and shape.

petals and leaves turn in an unseen breeze. The flipped underside of a petal shows the reverse of the fabric in a beautifully natural gesture. Striking realism characterizes classic Baltimore style. Roslyn's influence is to push us toward an even greater naturalism.

To produce her drawings as appliqués, Roslyn translated them into cottons (mostly solid colors) and embroidered them finely with telling detail.

With solids, the viewer's reading of scale is not adversely affected as can happen with prints. Her colors are clear, vivid, dramatic. Using sewing thread (either all-purpose sewing thread or machine embroidery thread, single strand) she combines a wealth of embroidery stitches with an artist's ease. Her basket (using Pattern #40 in the *Pattern Companion to Volume I)* was done with cut-away appliqué. The two decorative horizontal pieces were appliquéd on top as separate units. Jane Mitchell, co-owner of Sharon's Quilt Depot, credits Roslyn with inspiring a regional style distinguished by realistic botanical gesture, solid colors, and fine single-thread embroidered detail. But around Dallas, it is Roslyn's North American wildflowers more than her Australian ones that have captured Texan hearts. Her students have affectionately named her North American Wildflower Album, "The Texas Album."

Starched Pressing:
Roslyn's block has a flat, crisp look, much like the floral-appliquéd linens coming out of mainland China in recent years. Her ironing directions: Place the block face down on a square of muslin laid on a padded ironing board. Cover the back of the block with a second square of muslin. Now spray this overlaid muslin square (until wet) with Magic® Sizing and iron it with a hot, dry iron. Next turn the stack over and iron the right side of the block, protected by the muslin pressing square.

Rather than suggesting a specific alternate pattern, we issue you this lesson's challenge to take a Baltimore basket beautifully "beyond"!

LESSON 7

DIMENSIONAL WREATHS

The Wreath Challenge; Bias Stems: Two Ways: Superfine Stems I; Wreath Stems by Machine; Superfine Stems II; Crown of Ten Penny Roses; Crown of Quilted Roses; Straight-Stitched Leaves; Quilted Roses; Crown of Ruched Roses; Split Leaves and Other Fancies; Leaf Embellishments; Two-Color Ruching; Novelty Centers for Ruched Roses; Yo-Yo Center; Wool Turkeywork Center; Rolled Center Rose; French Knot Center; Finishing the Flower

PATTERN:
Crown of Ten Penny Roses, Pattern #4. See Color Plate 19. Crown of Quilted Roses, Pattern #5. See Color Plate 20. "Crown of Ruched Roses," Pattern #6. See Color Plate 26.

I have a dream about wreaths. Wreaths were favorites in the classic Albums, and, when there were enough of them, they affected a quilt's set. Wreaths are also an exceptionally easy and enticing format for playing with dimensional flowers.

The Wreath Challenge: The formula is simple: stems, leaves, and six to eight flowers per wreath. My dream is to take a memorable template (like a 9"-diameter dinner plate) to draw a wreath circle on each of 12 squares of background fabric. As part of the initial preparation, I'd machine stitch the folded bias to this circle (Superfine Stems I), then sit back to sew its outside perimeter by hand. My ambition is to concentrate on one dimensional flower type per wreath, thoroughly exploring its possibilities until I've learned a lot, had some fun, and am quite satisfied. Then I'd move on to the next wreath, the next flower. This lesson's block, "Crown of Ruched Roses," provoked this dream. By Lesson 10's end, you'll see that even more wreaths can be made studying ruching! And there is no end to other floral specimens. Perhaps you'll take the idea of "floral wreath studies" as another challenge and incorporate them in your Album.

BIAS STEMS: TWO WAYS

Superfine Stems I:
(Review the directions for these in *Volume I.)* How you mark the background is tied to how you make your stems. For each of the following methods, the background is marked differently. The dotted

CROWN OF TEN PENNY ROSES

placement line on this lesson's patterns emphasizes that you should mark the outside of the wreath, only, on your background block. This marking is for "Superfine Stems" taught in *Volume I.* Those stems, still my favorites, are perfect for this lesson's blocks. Alternatively, Marilyn Stem suggests the following refinement, which allows you to mark the stem's center line (rather than the outside line) and use the method for any width stem:

1. Cut a bias strip three times the width of your stem.

2. Draw one line only to mark the wreath on your background cloth: the lengthwise center line.

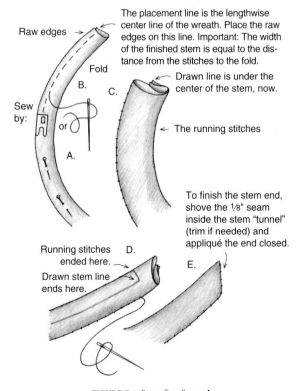

Raw edges →

The placement line is the lengthwise center line of the wreath. Place the raw edges on this line. Important: The width of the finished stem is equal to the distance from the stitches to the fold.

Fold

B.   C.

← Drawn line is under the center of the stem, now.

Sew by: or

← The running stitches

A.

Running stitches ended here. →   D.

Drawn stem line ends here. →

To finish the stem end, shove the 1/8" seam inside the stem "tunnel" (trim if needed) and appliqué the end closed.

E.

FIGURE 7-1. Superfine Stems I: Using a center placement line

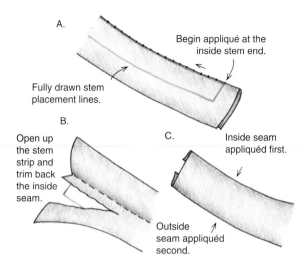

FIGURE 7-2. Superfine Stems II: Stems for a fully marked background

3. Fold the strip in half lengthwise, right sides out. Pin your stem strip so that the raw edge rests on the center line and the fold is to its right (Figure 7-1A). *Layering reminder:* Always place the stem strip ¼" or so into the area where the leaf (or other appliqué) will lie over it.

4. Righthanders, begin the actual sewing on the left stem of your crown wreath pattern. Starting at the top of the stem, take fine running stitches in a line that parallels the raw edge. This line should be one third of the distance from the raw edge to the fold (Figure 7-1B). The distance from the stitched line to the fold, then, becomes the width of the finished stem.

5. *The square base of the stem:* Continue your line of running stitches to the bottom end of the stem. Finish off your thread.

6. Finger-press the fold from right to left—against the stitched line, over the raw edges, to its resting place on the outside of the wreath. Pin it in place every two or three inches. Now appliqué the outside of the wreath from the top of the stem down (Figure 7-1C). *Note:* Very little of these stems show. If you want to speed the process up, place your leaves and flowers over the pinned stem and appliqué them in place. After you've sewn these motifs, you need only stitch the few inches of stem left uncovered.

7. *Completing the base of the stem:* Stop your appliqué stitches directly opposite your running stitches (where the pattern ends.) Trim

the seam bluntly to ¹⁄₁₆" beyond drawn stem end (Figure 7-1D). With embroidery scissors or a toothpick, stuff the seam allowance back up into the stem tunnel and stitch the stem closed (Figure 7-1E).

Wreath Stems by Machine:
Wreath stems are a great place to get some "plain sewing" done by machine. The running stitched seam for "Superfine Stems I" is well worth doing by machine, using the presser foot as a seam-width guide (Figure 7-1B, again). You could also make up a bunch of Lesson 4's turned-bias stems, a convenient stash ready for any wreath or bouquet. Simply mark the lengthwise center of the wreath stem for their placement.

Superfine Stems II
(for a Fully Marked Background):
These require carefully drawn parallel lines to mark the stem on the background fabric. Because excess seam allowance (needed for ease in the initial handling) is trimmed off in stages, the final stem is fine and flat.

1. Use a 1"-wide bias-cut strip folded in half lengthwise, right side out. (Ironing the fold is optional.)

2. Start at the bottom of the left stem of the crown. Pin the bias strip (fold to the center, raw edges toward the outside) so that its fold lies on top of the inside wreath line. Let the raw-edged tail of the strip fall ¼" below the penciled stem base (Figure 7-2A).

3. Appliqué the fold to the inside wreath stem line, beginning at the bottom. Start your appliqué stitches where the marking begins. This leaves the ¼" seam "hanging" below this point (Figure 7-2A, again).

4. When you've reached the top of the stem (¼" beyond the drawn line for layering), stop. Open the fold up and trim the underneath seam to ⅛" from the sewn fold (Figure 7-2B).

5. Now you'll appliqué the outside of the stem, sewing from the top down (Figure 7-2C). You'll be stretching the bias slightly to accommodate the widest part of the curve. You have two choices. You can tuck the full seam under, pushing any minimal excess inside to stuff the stem. Or you can trim a tiny bit off the raw edge for an even finer seam.

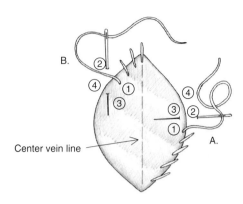

FIGURE 7-3. Straight-Stitched Leaves

TEXTURE AND COLOR IN REPEATED APPLIQUÉ MOTIFS: CROWN OF TEN PENNY ROSES

Currently, the quilt world is abuzz with the question of when a quilt is art, when it's not. At the bottom of the argument, it seems to me, the question is "What is art?" Immanuel Kant tackled that one, and the jury is still out. I put one college philosophy course, "Aesthetics," into trying to follow his and his fellow pundits' logic. I found it difficult. The question no longer burns for me. But the question of what gives a particular block a style intrigues me still. It's been much on my mind in dealing with dimensional flowers. It would be so easy, with all these elaborate flowers, to make the kind of overloaded offering that gives salad bars a bad name. One has to approach the design of a fancy flowers block with a strong sense of style, and often, the most exceptional blocks show great restraint. "Wreath of Ten Penny Roses" is such a block. It takes our wreath challenge formula at its most basic: stem, one leaf shape, and a circle the size of a dime. Artfully, these simple elements recur repeatedly over the block's surface.

Surprisingly simple, this block's rich lode of ore is color and texture, masterfully melded by Debbie Ballard. The color scheme is brilliant Baltimore: red and green contrasting vibrantly across from each other on the color wheel. But this block is a gold mine of texture, too. See all the texture in the prints and again in the wealth of rose petal fabrics—cottons, rayons, *crêpe de Chine,* jacquard silks. (Then just imagine how one might strike it rich with lush petals cut from closely shaded ribbons!) Two methods, covered earlier, will heighten your pleasure in designing these leaves and petals. They are "print windows" for the leaves from Lesson 1, and perfect circles for Quarter Roses from Lesson 4. Office dots (¾" circles) make super sticky-paper templates for pre-turning the circular petal's seam. Review Lesson 4's *caveats* (under "Quarter Roses") about sewing only that part of

the petal that shows, and removing one petal's template before proceeding on to the next. Other than coinage, these Ten Penny Roses and Quarter Roses differ only in the profile of their layout.

CROWN OF QUILTED ROSES

CROWN OF QUILTED ROSES

This refined-looking block offers a grand site on which to try out the "stem for a fully marked background." Its straight-stitched leaves were often sewn in wool, a "heavy" embroidery look, which was echoed in the embroidered quilting and edging on the roses.

Straight-Stitched Leaves:
In this style, the leaf's edge is straight-stitch embroidered, but no other appliqué stitch is used. Were I a betting woman, I'd say that originally the seams were basted under, the leaf was then basted to the block, the embroidery was done, then all that basting was removed. We can do it so much more easily now by pre-turning the seams over freezer paper or crack 'n peel (see Lesson 2). Double-pin or big-stitch baste these "hemmed" leaves to the block. Do the classic straight-stitch embroidery in two strands of embroidery floss. There is a detail of this stitch on the pattern. It is easier to stitch in one direction than the other. Wendy Grande offers these suggestions from her needlepoint background:

1. A righthanded person should begin at the bottom right side of the leaf. The stitch comes out of the leaf and into the background. When you point your needle to come out of the leaf again, point it straight at (perpendicular to) the center vein of the leaf (Figure 7-3A).

2. At the outer point of the leaf, the entering needle points straight ahead at (and takes a bite out of) the center vein line.

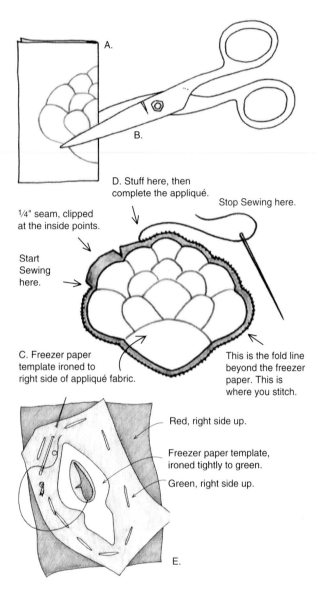

FIGURE 7-4. Quilting the Rose

3. Once past the point, on the left side, the entering needle is held parallel to the center vein line (Figure 7-3B).

4. *Removing the paper template:* Note that this straight stitch takes a substantial bite out of the leaf, and an even bigger one out of the background cloth. With tweezers and a slit from the back, you'll easily remove the template when you're finished. Loosen the seam first by reaching under and separating it from the paper with tweezers. When you're ready to pull the template out, pinch the appliqué's very edge to the background, to relieve stress on the actual stitches. Roll the tweezers as you pull the paper away from the stitches and out. Move your pinching tweezers along following the line of removal of the template.

Quilted Roses:

Stuffed, quilted roses are a distinctive, recurring style in the classic Album Quilts. When heavily embroidered, I think of them as "Dr. Dunton's Stuffed and Quilted Roses," for in his book, *Old Quilts,* William Rush Dunton describes them faithfully. A fine detail of an antique original is shown in the photographic detail of Quilt #10 in *Volume II's* Color Section.) In this series, these roses have been reproduced in polished cotton, or, here in Marjo Hodge's block, in silk *crêpe de Chine.* Gladys Clayson made lovely roses using a print window to cut them from chintz (Color Plate #8). Needleartists have made other patterns for these roses in three pieces, two pieces, or one piece. Since the roses in our lesson block are rather small, the simplest approach, a one-piece blossom, works beautifully. The needleturn (freezer paper on the top) method is best, for the paper stabilizes the highly mobile silk. Review Lesson 2 in *Volume I,* which teaches another sort of quilted rose. The procedure is basically the same, with the following exceptions:

Quilting the Rose:

You could trace both the appliqué rose shape and the petal-quilting marks directly onto the rose fabric. Then simply cut it out with seam allowances, double-pin to the block and needleturn. I chose to needleturn with freezer paper on the top and customized my template thus:

1. Fold a 3" square of freezer paper in half, coated sides inside. Open it to trace half the rose pattern (including the quilting lines) onto its left (uncoated) side. Refold and cut the rose out symmetrically (Figure 7-4A).

2. With the rose still folded, cut all the petal lines *partially* through, so that the template still holds together as one piece. This makes a perfectly symmetrical perforated quilting pattern (Figure 7-4B). It can be discarded in stages as each petal is quilted.

3. Iron this same freezer paper rose template to the right side of your red fabric. (Pre-test the fabric. Ironed too hot, or too forcefully, freezer paper can stick "permanently" to both silk and polished cotton.) Needleturn the seam under around it, leaving an unsewn space on the upper left (Figure 7-4C).

4. Pull off the template covering the large bottom petal. Using something narrow and blunt (a crochet hook or an orange cuticle stick) push a half teaspoon of polyester fiber

down into the base of the rose. Embroider the curved base petal line. Use a back stitch to quilt through appliqué, filler, and backing. Use either silk buttonhole twist or one strand of embroidery floss in a color matched to the rose. Work your way up the rose, peeling off paper petals, stuffing, and embroidering-quilting as you go. When you've quilted all but the uppermost row of petals, close up the opening left in the seam (Figure 7-4D). Embroider the finished rose in chain or outline stitch.

6. For the bud, reverse appliqué the bud calyx (marked by a freezer paper template on top) to a swatch of red cloth (Figure 7-4E). When the bud is sewn, turn to the wrong side, and trim the red back to within ⅛" of its seamline.

7. From the front, trim the unsewn green seam to 3/16" of the freezer paper. Needleturn the calyx to the block. You can back-stitch quilt around the bud. Then slit the quilted background cloth behind the bud to stuff it. Embroider the bud as detailed on the pattern.

CROWN OF RUCHED ROSES

CROWN OF RUCHED ROSES

Split Leaves and Other Fancies:
By now, a quiltmaker using the *Baltimore Beauties* series has fine taste in leaf greens, verdant prints, plains, and the combinations thereof. I'm partial to yellowy greens, called "Victoria Green" during that late queen's reign. But rather than stay solely with a single tone, our foliage needs the depth of both light and dark to capture the mottling of natural sunshine through leaves. Any block benefits from sporting a spectrum of tint saturations. These propel the viewer from the calm evoked by pale colors to the excitement created by pulsingly rich intensities of hue. The subtly stepped grades of

hand-dyed shades, tie-dyed and marbelized fabrics, the occasional geometric, and large prints cut-up, now characterize our Album Quilt palettes. In addition, leaves, which are split in half down the center (a design conceit culled from antique Albums), add depth and realism to our greenery. Try these variations:

1. Machine two strips of cloth (each 1½"-wide) together with a ⅛" seam (Figure 7-5A). Beth Martin suggests one print be right side up, stripped to the wrong side up of the same print. Used side by side, this combination adds depth and a cohesive color variation to the leaves. To give a vertical print the diagonal look of leaf veins, she cut the strips on the bias (Figure 7-5B).

2. Moiré prints have a linear quality and make eye-catching leaves. Any linear green print can be cut on the bias for stripped leaves with a veined effect. When you pin the two strips together, line the diagonals up so they form a "V" effect at the seam line (Figure 7-5C). With the seams pressed over freezer paper, a leaf is well-defined for color placement on the block.

Leaf Embellishments:
The leaf vein lines on "Crown of Ruched Roses" have been top-stitched in a single strand of No. 50 machine embroidery thread. (Top-stitching is a quilting stitch through both the appliqué and the background fabric.) The edges of the leaves are embroidered, either with a straight-stitch or a blanket stitch whose "leg" extends out into the background fabric in rhythmically upward-reaching diagonals (Figure 7-5D).

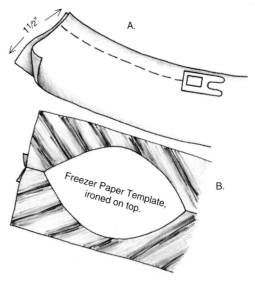

FIGURE 7-5. Split Leaves

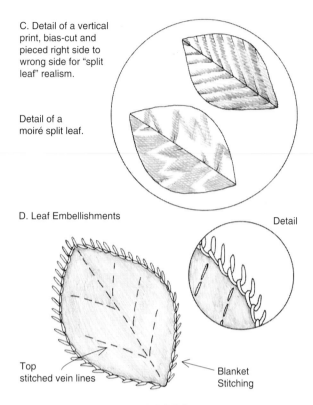

C. Detail of a vertical print, bias-cut and pieced right side to wrong side for "split leaf" realism.

Detail of a moiré split leaf.

D. Leaf Embellishments

Detail

Top stitched vein lines

Blanket Stitching

FIGURE 7-5. Split Leaves

Two-Color Ruching:

A wee photograph of a classic Album block inspired me to make "Crown of Ruched Roses" with its variegated ruching. It captured my imagination. In both the new and the old, the colors change from the rim of each flower to its center. Use the right angle sewing (See Ruching Pattern I in Lesson 9). For our crown's roses, modify *Volume I's* ruching instructions in the following areas:

1. *Cutting the cloth strip for ruching:* To begin this block, I chose a handful of silk and rayon fabrics in close shades. When you enrich a rose by starting it in one color strip and finishing it in another, you want the hue transition to be subtle. For the informal multi-colored ruching I favor, cut the strips 1¼" wide and any length from 10" to 20" long. Plan on two to three strips per flower. Because you simply add another strip when the first one runs out, this method needs no calculation of total length per flower. If you use a soft synthetic or silk, cut the cloth on the straight. It's more economical. But if you use cotton or a poly-cotton, cut the strip on the bias. Then it bends to the curves more easily and avoids ungainly bulk. Ruche the full length of several strips before you begin sewing the first one to the background.

Note: Some rare antebellum Album flowers were, in fact, ruched in discrete rows of color. Blooms of three concentric rows of blue, yellow, and red stick in my memory. (I noted to myself that flower's symbolic color triumvirate. It is the same as the cornucopias' links or the freedom caps' stripes.) But the very infrequency of such precise coloration bespeaks the figuring required to reproduce the look.

2. *Sewing Begins on the Outside of the Rose:* Draw the pattern's placement circle on the background fabric. Baste the lengthwise center of the first ruched strip along this pencil line. Tuck its beginning "tail" inward, about ½", toward the center (Figure 7-6A). Basting with flower-colored thread, take short stitches on the top, longer ones underneath. These stitches stay in. When you begin the second row, overlap its outer petals to the mid-line (the gathering line) of the first row of petals (Figure 7-6B).

3. *Changing Colors:* When the first ruched strip runs out, tuck its tail diagonally in toward the center (Figure 7-6C). To begin the next color strip, lay its tail crosswise over the previous strip's tail end (Figure 7-6D). Resume basting the center line. How far in should you ruche for our novel centers? It varies. End the last ruched strip anywhere from leaving an open center the size of a quarter (Figure 7-6E) to having the ruching brush against itself in the center. Tucked fringe adorns these filled centers well. Yo-Yos, French knots, or Turkeywork complete wider center expanses. Try to select a ruched strip that runs out at the right place. But if need be, you can cut a ruched strip short. To do this, pull stitches out, put the thread in a needle, and backstitch where you want to cut the strip. Or machine stay stitch through the hand gathering, then trim off the excess.

Novelty Centers for Ruched Roses:

The various blossom centers are numbered in a key on Pattern #6. The easiest center is Mrs. Numsen's Fringed Center from Lesson 2. In Blossom #1, it is made of a rich gold China silk and tucked into a Yo-Yo center of pink to red hand-dyed silk. The fringe in Blossom #5 is corn-silk-colored cotton.

Yo-Yo Center (Blossoms #1 and #2): Using the Yo-Yo template (Figure 7-7A), cut a circle of quilt-

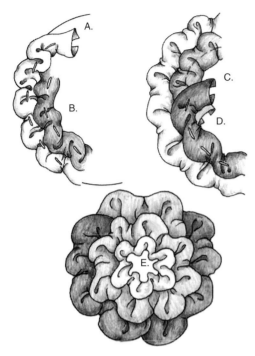

FIGURE 7-6. Two Color Ruching

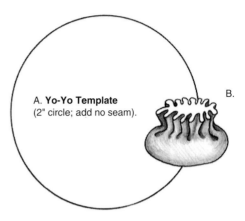

FIGURE 7-7. Yo-Yo Center

weight cloth. Stitch a ¼" hem around its outer edge. Place the stitches closer to the raw edge than to the fold. When you pull the thread to gather it, a ruff is formed (Figure 7-7B). Make the Yo-Yo circle larger if you need to fill more space in the flower's center. I chose contrasting fabrics for these Yo-Yo centers and filled the top one with a fringe. Tuck the Yo-Yo into the flower's center. Adjust its position before sewing it down. Mine are pushed slightly up and to the side so that a bit of the base shows in front of the ruffles.

- *Variations:* Lou Fortney suggests leaving the Yo-Yo circle unhemmed (raw-edged) and inserting a yellow stamen fringe. This makes a light and charming flower.

- Another variation is to fringe ¼" of the Yo-Yo circle's raw edge, then make a running stitch ⅓" inside this circle. When you pull to gather, a Yo-Yo made this way will already have a fringed center.

- A flower can quickly be finished with a same-colored Yo-Yo, rather than making another ruched strip to fill the remaining space. (The impression then given is that the whole flower is ruched.)

Wool Turkeywork Center (Blossom #3): Thread an 18" piece of golden crewel wool into a crewel needle. Fill the flower center with ½"-long loops. Trim the top of the loops off so that the center is a fuzz of raw yarn ends.

Rolled Rose Center (Blossom #4): If you looked at the Color Section and guessed that this fourth blossom used up the last pre-ruched strip and left a large hole in the center, you're right. I filled that empty space with a Rolled Silk Rose. This was made using a 1¼"-wide straight-cut strip of silk hand-dye. This is basically "rolled ruching" and follows Rolled Rose Method #2: Lengthwise-Folded and Double-Edge-Gathered Strip; directions are in Lesson 1.

French Knot Center (Blossom #6): Use six strands of yellow cotton embroidery floss threaded in a crewel needle to fill a flower center with a chunky crowd of French knots.

Lesson 1's three rolled-rose methods (done in cloth) would make a lively wreath study in themselves. If such an undertaking appeals, Method #2 (where the lengthwise fold itself is gathered) offers rich variations. Some of these are: using a plaid taffeta ribbon (suggested by Virginia Earhart); using a straight-cut raw-edged cotton or rayon strip with both margins slightly fringed (Lisa Schiller); using a raw-edged bias strip; pinking a straight-cut strip. (Did you know that pinking shears come with scallop-edged as well as triangle-edged blades? The petite scallops they make are delightful!)

Finishing the Flower:
A 1¼"-wide strip is ideal for floral ruching. When you fold the lengthwise edges into the center, make them overlap by about ⅛". These edges will stay tucked under nicely. Unless they are straight cut and fray badly, appliqué just the outer rim of petals down. Were the ruching strip cut 1" wide, each petal in each exposed row would have to be tacked down. Leaving petals unsewn makes a more sculptural flower.

For more wreaths, go on to Lesson 8.

LESSON 8

FANCY FLOWERS INTERPRETED

Rick Rack Roses; Cleda's Rick Rack Blooms; Painting Rick Rack and Ribbon; Pleated Flowers; Gathered Leaves; Petals-on-a-String; Mrs. Numsen's Rose I

PATTERNS:

"Rick Rack Roses," Pattern #7. See Color Plate 37. "Baltimore Bouquet," Pattern #21. See Color Plate 33. "I Promised You a Rose Garden," Pattern #2. See Color Plate 34.

Quilter's Newsletter Magazine published my article on "Fancy Flowers" over three issues in 1990-'91. It taught the dimensional flowers in Lesson 9's Pattern #24. The previous year, *QNM* had published another of my articles, "The Numsen Quilt: Fancy Flowers from Old Baltimore." That article introduced some techniques for Lesson 10's "Beribboned Bouquets." Glorious flowers have germinated from those articles' seeds! Gwendolyn LeLacheur, a talented quiltmaking teacher from Harsen's Island, Michigan, took off on some of those floral methods, along with some of her own in designing "beyond Baltimore" blocks. Her style is dynamic, distinctive, and appealing. She designed this Lesson's three patterns and generously shares them here. They give us a relaxing arena for learning more techniques and ease us into methods used in the more complex blocks of Lessons 9 and 10.

RICK RACK ROSES: STITCHED AND PAINTED

Rick rack roses seemed so "out of the 1950s" that I hesitated about leaving them in the "Fancy Flowers" block for an Album Quilt with 19th-century antecedents. I'm told that rick rack actually comes from the 1920s. While this lively trim rises and falls in fashion, it now seems clear that many would like to capitalize on its perky realism for roses.

Old 100%-cotton rick rack is the nicest, but polyester blends work, too. Rick rack comes in multiple sizes: small, medium, large, jumbo, and oversized. More common sizes are available prepackaged; the largest size is available off the spool, by the yard. The diameter of the finished flower can be varied both by the width of the rick rack used and by the length of the strip used. Standard red rick rack works perfectly for Gwen LeLacheur's blooms in Pattern #7. Jumbo rick rack, 1¼ yards of it, is needed per blossom:

RICK RACK ROSES

1. *Braiding rick rack:* Hold the length of rick rack folded in half in your left hand. With your right hand, wind one half of the strip in front of, then behind, the other strip which is stationary. Repeat this "braiding" so that the points of one strip link into the valleys of the other (Figure 8-1A). When completely braided, pin the bottom of the strip to hold the braid.

2. Next, roll this braided strip four times around the folded end where you started. Wrap tightly to form the rose's center petals (Figure 8-1B). The bottom will be flat with all the points at one level. Sew this base by whipstitching one row to another with red thread. For this large rose, continue wrapping and whipstitching until the unused braid is about 10" long. Secure the last stitches.

3. Now sew gathering stitches (one in and out of each point) at the inner edge of the strip (Figure 8-1C). Pull thread to gather gently and wind this strip around the bud base's outer ridge, forming its more open outer petals.

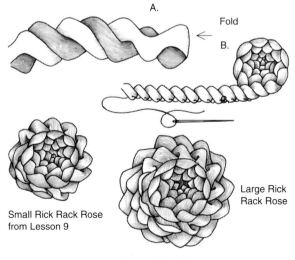

FIGURE 8-1. Rick Rack Roses

4. Overcast the outer petal points to the bud base. Tuck under the raw-edged end so that it is hidden under the flower. Secure your last stitches. If there is any excess length of braid, trim it off to adjust the flower's size.

Cleda's Rick Rack Blooms:
Cleda Dawson hybridized a beautiful two-tone rick rack flower whose radiating quill-like petals remind one of a dahlia. It is the uppermost of the four large blossoms in Color Plate #29. To imitate that flower:

1. Place 12" of yellow rick rack on top of 12" of goldenrod-colored rick rack. Put a pin through the first set of points. Braid the length and pin the ends together (see Figure 8-1A, again).

3. Hold the braid in your left hand. With a double thread in gold, sew the outside row—the row facing away from you. Put a stitch into one point and have it come out of the next point, and so on (Figure 8-1C, again).

4. Pull to gather the braid. Leave the thread unsecured so that you can re-pull the gathers at the end of the thread when they have loosened.

5. Draw a 1½" circle on your background cloth. Thread another needle, double. With the raw-edged tail pinned just inside the circle, whipstitch the inner row of points to the line (Figure 8-2A). How tight should the gathers be before you stitch them down? The point of a gold one should overlap the point of the yellow one to its left by about half.

Painting Rick Rack or Ribbon:
Maggie Dupuis, frustrated by the limited color range in polyester rick rack, found both fabric paint and a method for customizing synthetic trim into elegant flora:

1. Use Deka® permanent fabric paint in a shade darker than the rick rack.

2. Rub the paint onto the rick rack laid on paper. (You can even do this spotty painting with a rubber-gloved fingertip, rinsing it to change colors.) To keep the rick rack flexible, keep the paint layer thin.

3. The color can be made to bleed so that it shades artistically into the rick rack's color. First, let the paint dry for about an hour.

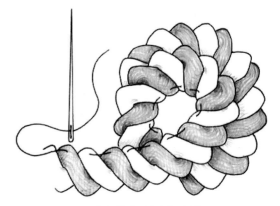

FIGURE 8-2. Cleda's Rick Rack Blooms

Then lay the rick rack in a shallow dish in the sink, lifting it up when the color reaches the desired soft-edged, painterly effect.

4. Let the rick rack dry, then iron to heat-set according to the manufacturer's directions. Protect your iron with a press cloth.

Pleated Flowers:
Pleated flowers go back to the old Album Quilts and beyond. Botanically non-specific, they are simply, poetically suggestive. Elongated, they make me think of Trumpet Vine flowers, summer, and the seashore. The technique is full of possibilities. (In the wreath studies suggested in Lesson 7, pleated flowers, 1¾" deep in lush-colored shades, would be showy.) Gwen fashioned wee charming pleated blossoms thus:

1. For Pattern #7, cut a 1" x 2½" rectangle of cotton cloth. Iron under a 3/16" hem on the top and sides (Figure 8-3A). To hold the hem, and then to hold the pleats, use a bit of liquid starch dabbed from the wrong side onto the seam. Or, suggests Gwen, use a strand of ThreadFuse™ laid inside each fold and pressed to bond it.

2. Accordion-pleat the hemmed rectangle into four pleats. Iron each pleat to press the creases in (Figure 8-3B).

3. Tuck the bottom of the pleated rectangle into the flower's open calyx (Figure 8-3B). Fan the pleats out a bit at the top of the bloom and appliqué in place.

Annie's Pleated Flowers:
A clever notion, Clotilde's Perfect Pleater®, makes pleating a snap. It is a roughly notebook-page-sized rectangle of rigid pleated cloth, which pins to the ironing board. You tuck the fabric into the pleats and steam press (or spray starch) them into

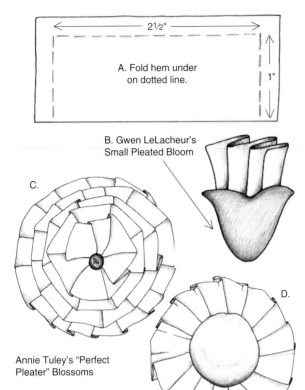

A. Fold hem under
on dotted line.

2½"

1"

B. Gwen LeLacheur's
Small Pleated Bloom

C.

D.

Annie Tuley's "Perfect
Pleater" Blossoms

FIGURE 8-3 Pleated Flowers

the cloth. You can make "yards" of ¼", ½", ¾" (or wider) pleats. Or combine sizes. Annie Tuley, used the Perfect Pleater® to make several versions of her pleated basket, Pattern #28. She also shares the following directions for two kinds of pleated flowers from her "Blue Album" Quilt #2 in the Color Section. Annie sewed hers by machine.

1. Straight-cut a 2"-wide strip by 44" (or the width of the yardage).

2. Fold it in half, lengthwise, and pleat it every ¼".

3. Draw a 1⅓" base on the background cloth. Iron a piece of freezer paper to the back of the cloth to stabilize it while machine sewing.

4. Place the right end of the strip just inside the drawn circle to hide the tail. The fold is on the left of the line, outside it; the raw edges are on the line. Stitch the pleated strip to the line with zigzag stitches in invisible thread. Spiral inward, placing each subsequent row ⅛" farther toward the center. In the center, tuck the raw-edged end under (at a right angle) to hide it. Annie sews a bead (or

beads) at the center. Mrs. Numsen's fringed center would finish this bloom nicely as well (Figure 8-3C).

5. The second variation has just an outer row of the same pleats as before. Thus it needs a larger (1⅓" without seams) center circle stuffed and sewn to cover the ruff's raw edges. This flower would make a great sunflower with French knot seeds (or beads) adorning its plump middle (Figure 8-3D).

BALTIMORE BOUQUET

BALTIMORE BOUQUET

Gwen's Gathered Leaves:

1. Cut a bias strip 2" wide and 9" long. Run the strip through a 1" bias-tape maker to fold the raw edges under.

2. Cut the bias strip into three 3" lengths. To make a leaf, finger-press a 1" hem at the top end of the leaf. Fold the left and right edges into the center as if making a prairie point (Figure 8-4).

3. Gather along the bottom edge. Secure the stitches. Trim off the excess fabric at bottom. Appliqué with seam-side down.

Petals-On-A-String:

1. Trace around a 25¢ coin. Cut out a circle on this drawn line.

2. Fold the circle (right sides out) into quarters.

3. Sew close to the raw edges through all the layers. Do not cut the thread. Make another circle. Repeat steps 1 and 2, then add this petal onto the string (Figure 8-5).

4. Make a total of five circles. Draw them into a circle, connecting the first and the last petal. Secure the thread. The fold of each

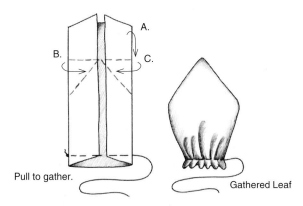

Pull to gather.

Gathered Leaf

FIGURE 8-4. Gathered Leaves

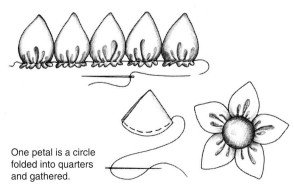

One petal is a circle
folded into quarters
and gathered.

FIGURE 8-5. Petals-on-a-String

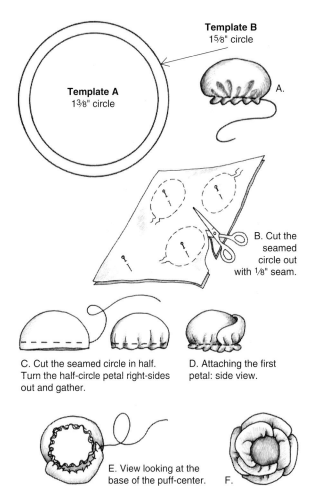

Template B
1⅝" circle

Template A
1⅜" circle

A.

B. Cut the
seamed
circle out
with ⅛" seam.

C. Cut the seamed circle in half.
Turn the half-circle petal right-sides
out and gather.

D. Attaching the first
petal: side view.

E. View looking at the
base of the puff-center.

F.

FIGURE 8-6. Mrs. Numsen's Puff-Centered Rose

petal should be on the same side. Sew in place along the inside leaving the petals free. Fill the centers with an appliquéd circle.

I PROMISED YOU A ROSE GARDEN

Mrs. Numsen's Rose I:
Gwen LeLacheur's instructions for these follow. She used three closely related shades of hand-dyed cotton for each rose. The effect is lovely. We'll dub these shades as colors #1, 2, and 3.

1. *Center circle:* cut one circle (1⅜" diameter) from color #1. Use Template A for this and cut on the drawn line (Figure 8-6). Sew a gathering stitch ⅛" inside the circle's edge. Tug to gather these stitches forming a pouch (Figure 8-6A).

2. Stuff this pouch firmly with polyester fiber. Pull thread to gather the pouch into a tight, button-like mushroom cap shape and secure the stitches.

3. *Petals #1, 2, and 3:* Pin together two 4" squares (cut on grain) of color #1, right sides together. Draw three Template A circles, leaving room for a ⅛" seam around each. Pin inside each circle. Machine seam the two layers together, sewing the circle's drawn line in a fine stitch. Cut the circles out ⅛" beyond the sewn line (Figure 8-6B).

4. Now cut each of these circles in half, on the straight of grain. Turn them right side out.

5. Take small running stitches along each petal's straight-cut edge (Figure 8-6C). Pull these stitches gently so that this "petal" cups slightly to conform to the center puff (Figure 8-6D).

6. Attach petals #1, 2, and 3, overlapping each slightly as you sew them around the puff center. Keep all the raw edges at the same level on the back so that the base is flat. Put three petals in the first round, closest to the center puff. Stitch the petals to the center, holding the bloom upside down (Figure 8-6E).

7. The second (and last) row has four overlapping petals made from color #3. To make petals #4, 5, 6, and 7, use Template B (a 1⅝" circle) and repeat steps 3, 4, 5, and 6. Stitch these last petals, through their bases, tightly to the inner row of petals. The back of the flower stays flat. It sits firmly on the quilt block (Figure 8-6F). Stitch its perimeter to the background fabric. This is a beautiful flower with further variants given in Lesson 10.

Embellishments:

Gwen has made embroidered embellishment a hallmark of her style. Her camel-colored embroidery floss (one strand) creates a tracery throughout her designs in French knots, stem, chain, and blanket stitches. The blanket stitch characteristically is done with the leg of the stitch into the background rather than into the leaf. The latter softens the edges of the leaves, suggesting botanical realism, and, by its color, giving an antique richness to the blocks.

Another Gwendolyn LeLacheur design, which you can make: "Roses are Red," Pattern #1.

LESSON 9

ADVANCED BLOOMS: FILLING A VASE WITH FANCY FLOWERS

Small Rick Rack Roses; Making a Ruched Flower "in Hand"; Shell Ruching, Heart-Monitor Ruching, and Coin Ruching; Half-Ruching; Strip-Pieced Ruching; Ruched Circles; Larkspur; Ruched Calyxes; Ruched Buds

PATTERN:
"Fancy Flowers," Pattern #24A and B. See Color Plate 32.

An exuberant block caught my eye. It stayed with me until I made one of my own. What I saw was a vase of flowers picked freely by the imagination, and set quite casually into a vase as though all this stitching could easily be done afresh, tomorrow. The arrangement was pleasing and informal in that first block. Its maker was having fun, harvesting summer's first blooms from a luxuriant bed of fancy flowers. It seems she was making "something for herself."

That prototype block looks as fresh as ever. It's block A-1 in *Volume II's* Quilt #10. Picking my bouquet in the same summery mood, my vase came out quite differently. And it is that fecund season's atmosphere, most of all, that this lesson has to offer you. Its field of flowers includes a full block pattern, which you can follow. It is filled with blossoms all of whose lessons you have learned by this stage in the book. A legend on the pattern indexes where each technique is taught. You could repeat this pattern in a marvelous recital of each of those techniques. Or you could look at both blocks, hers and mine, and pick, for your block, a bouquet all your own.

Choose this block's vase pattern or pattern 24B, the original antebellum Album's vase. The vessel's shape, then its color, then the stems are your first decisions in making a block for this lesson. The other choices can be made as you go. My vase came from the border of a quilt dated 1856. I left its mouth unsewn, temporarily. This I filled with unadorned stems arranged in a rough six-inch radius from the center. The original block's maker embroidered her stems, possibly first penciling them on the cloth. Even 150 years later, this is an advanced block. It invites you to do it your way. Specific notes for this block follow, and then there is a special section on newly rediscovered ruching techniques.

FANCY FLOWERS

SMALL RICK RACK FLOWERS

The basic instructions for these are in Lesson 8. For this block's smaller flowers, use 12" of medium-sized red rick rack, folded in half and "braided." Roll the center four to five times round before gathering the last 1½" into the bud. This gathered 1½" row forms a ruff of open petals around the tight, upright center bud.

RUCHED FLOWERS MADE-IN-HAND

Follow the basic ruching instructions from *Volume I*, Lesson 8. Those are for a ruched flower constructed on the background cloth. You can make this vase's ruched flowers, each with a perfectly formed center, in your hand. Use a strip of seam tape, ½" x 20". Match your sewing thread to the seam tape. Take running stitches in right angle zigzags from folded edge to folded edge. (Figure 9-1A shows how to mark the ruching pattern, if desired.) Next:

1. Sew five inches of the seam tape, then pull to gather the stitches. Each triangle becomes a shell-like petal. Continue stitching and gathering until the whole 18" is ruched. A series of shell-like triangular puffs results. Park your needle at the end of the strip. Don't end off the thread yet (Figure 9-1B).

2. *To form the center:* Hold the ruched strip in your left hand. With a second needle, stitch a gathering thread in and out of each of the four bottom petals (Figure 9-1B).

3. Fold the wreath of four inner petals and the five outer petals in half (right sides together) like a fan, as in Figure 9-1C. (The tail is pressed back toward you, over the wrong side of outer petal #1.) Pull the gathering thread tightly. Backstitch to hold the four center petals together.

4. With the same thread, tack-stitch the left of inner petal #1 to the valley between outer petals #5 and #6 (Figure 9-1D).

5. Flatten the blossom's center and begin appliquéing its outside petals to the center of the row pulled under it. Sew outer petals #1 and #2 to outer petal #6 (Figure 9-1E).

6. Keep sewing the outside petals of one row to the center gathering line of the next row. This covers that next row's inner petals. Tack-stitch five or so stitches per petal.

7. Pull the second raw-edged tail under when you come to it, and secure it to finish. You can make even large (3" diameter and more) flowers in your hands. Making these as separate units means you can make them before placing them on the background. This opens up a wealth of design possibilities. *Note:* In general, when the ruching strip is wider, more petals have to be pulled in to form a flower center.

THREE DISTINCTIVE RUCHING PATTERNS — AND MORE

There is even more to ruching. Ruching can be done in three different gathering patterns. Each has a quite different effect, lots of floral potential, and each is striking. The impact comes in the careful repetition of the ruching pattern. Try these out in one-half to one-yard lengths of 1" wire ribbon (remove the wire). What follows takes you beyond "Fancy Flowers." But if fancy flowers in wreaths, or vases, or bouquets inspire you, perhaps you'll make a place to use one of the following suggestions.

Ruching Pattern I. Shell Ruching
(Figure 9-2A): To fold the zigzag ruching pattern, hold the raw end in your left hand and fold the ribbon down at a right angle. Continue folding right angles for the length of the ribbon. Then stitch the ruching line along the folds, gathering as you go. As shown in Figure 9-1, each triangle results in a shell-like puff.

Ruching Pattern II. Heart-Monitor Ruching
(Figure 9-2B): This can be done by sewing inside the bottom selvage for 1", then sewing an acute triangle up to the top selvage, looping the thread over and repeating the stitching pattern. When pulled, this stitching gives you a full round petal on one side of the ribbon strip only. If you wanted to make the outside petals of a flower bigger, you could stitch along the selvage at 1" intervals for seven repeats, then stitch at 1½" intervals, and so forth. Increasing the interval distance increases the fullness of the petals.

Ruching Pattern III. Coin Ruching
Using a quarter, draw circles the length of the strip as shown in Figure 9-2C. Note that the circle skims the inside of the bottom selvage, and turns into a straight line looping over the top selvage,

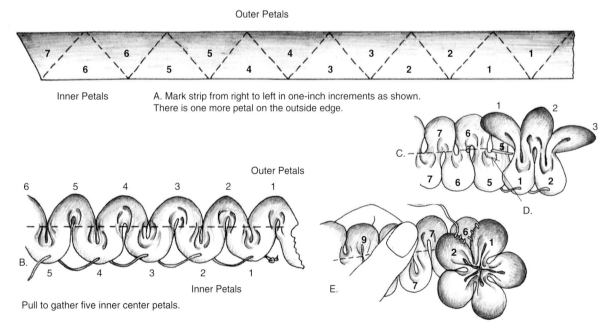

Outer Petals

7   6   5   4   3   2   1

6   5   4   3   2   1

Inner Petals   A. Mark strip from right to left in one-inch increments as shown. There is one more petal on the outside edge.

Outer Petals

6   5   4   3   2   1

B.

5   4   3   2   1

Inner Petals

Pull to gather five inner center petals.

C.

D.

E.

FIGURE 9-1. Ruched Flowers Made In-Hand

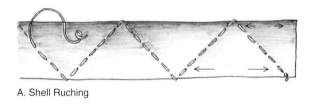

A. Shell Ruching

B. Heart Monitor Ruching

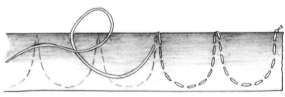

C. Coin Ruching

FIGURE 9-2. Three Ruching Patterns

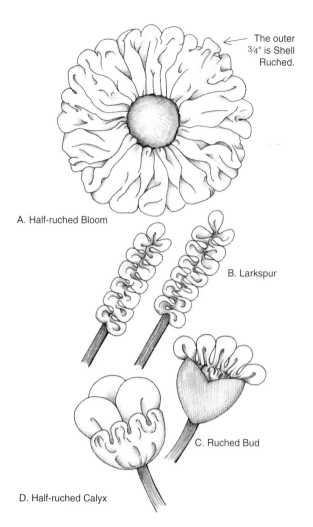

A. Half-ruched Bloom

B. Larkspur

C. Ruched Bud

D. Half-ruched Calyx

← The outer ¾" is Shell Ruched.

FIGURE 9-3. Half-Ruching and Other Uses for Shell-Ruching

making the actual repeat a "U" shape. Stitched and pulled this makes a charming pattern of generous puffs on the top side and petite ones on the bottom. You're sure to see a beguiling flower reflected in its ruffles. Five outer petals, for example, pulled into a wreath, make what an Asilomar class dubbed a "Wendy Rose" (named for Wendy Grande, my teaching assistant, who created that rose).

HALF-RUCHING AND OTHER VARIATIONS ON SHELL-RUCHING SUGGESTIONS

"Half-Ruching" is a delightful method suggested both by Dalphene Parks and Sue Linker. To make a 3"-diameter flower (Figure 9-3A):

1. Cut a rectangle of cotton 2½" x 22". Hem the top edge under ¾". Press this hem to the wrong side of the strip.

2. Ruche the hemmed ¾" edge of the rectangle in a ½"-deep zigzag pattern. Pull thread together after ruching every 5" or so.

3. Take gathering stitches through the bottom edge. Pull tightly to form a circle. Appliqué one short end of the rectangle over the other. Appliqué the ruched circumference to the background.

4. Appliqué a 1¼" circle (including seams) over the center.

Dalphene also suggests 3" lengths of ruching atop a stem for larkspur (Figure 9-3B). Salle Crittenden suggests ruched buds for the ruched roses (Figure 9-3C). And Melody Bollay suggests half-ruched calyxes (Figure 9-3D). Karen Poll suggests Strip-Pieced Ruching: Seam two different color strips, each 1" wide, down the center. When the center seam is pressed open and the long sides pressed into the center, you can shell-ruche it. Each flower petal it produces is edged in the second color. Sue Linker suggests ruching a 5" circle to make a 2¼"-diameter flower. She writes that if you press under a ¾" hem all around, the result is a dome. To make it flower-like, use a running stitch around a circle the size of a quarter in the center. Pull thread to gather. If you have a high-tech sewing machine, try ruching with a serpentine stitch at its widest. The very air is pulsing with ruched flowers to be made!

Another pattern, which could be filled with more fancy flowers: "Vase of Full-Blown Roses I," Pattern #10.

LESSON 10

ADVANCED BLOOMS:
BERIBBONED BOUQUETS

Mrs. Numsen's Rose II; Beribboned Bouquet; Mrs. Numsen's Rose III; Floribunda Rose; Ruching a Ribbon Camelia; Foxgloves or Bluebells; Primroses; Lilies of the Valley; Puff-Centered Peony Bud; Red Wire Ribbon Posies; Christmas Cactus Bud; A Symbolic Bouquet

PATTERN:
Numsen Family Bouquet Revisited, Pattern #22. See Color Plate 24. Beribboned Bouquet, also Pattern #22. See Color Plate 23.

Volume III focuses on a lively Album Quilt, folk-art free with fancy flowers and cross-stitched with Numsen family names. My fascination with this quilt, this family, was first told in a *Quilter's Newsletter Magazine* article (1/90). Our lesson pattern is one I drafted, based on a bouquet in that quilt. Nancy Hornback, a quilt scholar and needlewoman, made a lovely interpretation of it, and I did another, writing my block's techniques up in *Threads* Magazine (12/92). Both are pictured in the Color Section. Pattern #22 has a key that shows which techniques are used. Many of these blooms you've learned in prior lessons. Several are new and are taught here.

Our quilt world thrives on challenges. How two needleartists, working separately from the same pattern, envision and approach the block totally differently is a challenge. Perhaps you'd like to carry it on from Nancy's and my beginnings. Or perhaps the challenge of manipulating blooming bouquets in blocks of your own design, appeals. I designed this block's pattern to be done by cut-away appliqué. You could easily design bouquets of your own with bunches of pre-turned stems. In that case, two further items of information might be useful: First, the same 6" radius, which bounds a basket's blooms, works well for a bouquet. (Our needlesisters of old Baltimore sometimes balanced the stem half of the block with a bow and a bird, blossom, or butterfly.) Second, you can literally tie a ribbon (or cut cloth) around your bouquet's stems, then appliqué it down. Various versions of this, antique and modern, abound. Tying timeless bouquets is great fun! When you design your bouquet on the block, consider that it can be vertical or diagonal as your quilt's needs dictate. And we have precedent from

NUMSEN FAMILY BOUQUET REVISITED

old Baltimore: Not all blossoms need a stem; not all leaves touch a stem; not all stems need to reach the bow. Keep your bouquets light and airy, and they will bloom another century and more!

About This Lesson's Block Models:
"Numsen Family Bouquet Revisited," (Color Plate #24) by Nancy Hornback is based on Leaf/Stem Pattern #22. It is a quiet version of my block (Color Plate #23), which uses the same leaf/stem foundation. Nancy's is charmingly consistent: The same-weight cotton and pleasingly limited palette are used throughout. Just one print (a green calico) and four solids impart soft restraint. Each same-species flower shares just one color, clustering them with a reassuring sameness. In my "Beribboned Bouquet," even the ribbon pushes restraint. The primroses on the lower left have different centers and seem more fantasy than real. Three flowers in Nancy's bouquet differ in technique from my interpretation of this same pattern. These are: 1. The deep red chrysanthemum ruched of cotton (a bias cut strip 1⅛" x 40"); 2. The folded blossoms (Folded-Circle Rosebuds from *Volume I*); and 3. The bright yellow Mrs. Numsen's Rose II, made of half circles surrounding a puff center. Directions follow for these roses, and then for the flowers in my block. Several of the blooms in my block have been taught in earlier lessons: the open rose and the folded rose in Lesson 1 and the tucked circle (here a 1" circle) rosebuds from Lesson 8.

Mrs. Numsen's Rose II:
This is a second version of Lesson 8's Mrs. Numsen's Rose.

1. *The Rose's Petals.* For the outer petals: Cut seven circles 2¼" in diameter. For the inner petals (including the center one): Cut six circles 1⅞" in diameter (Figure 10-1A).

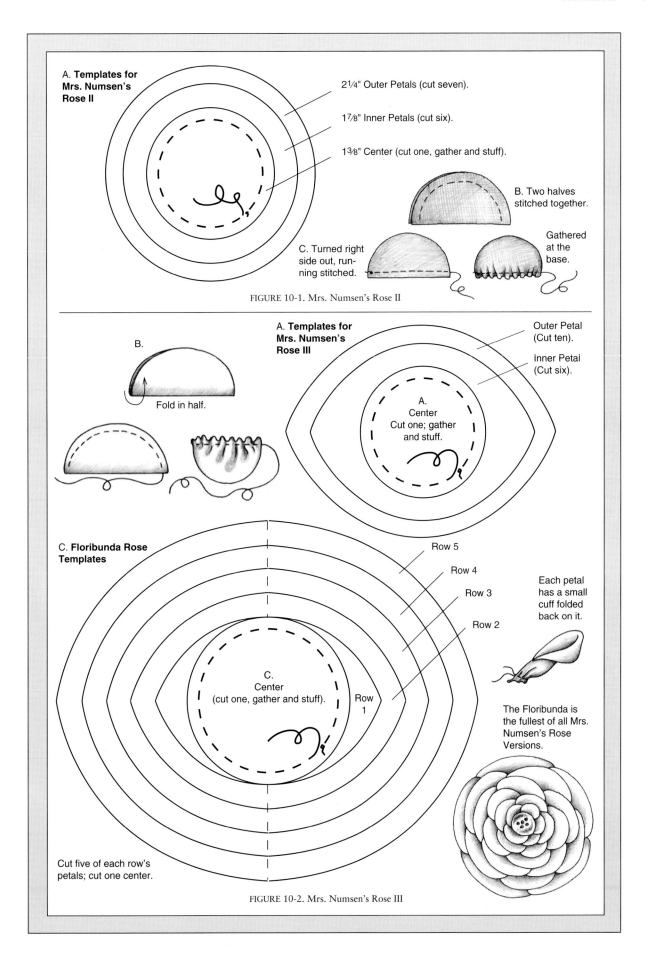

A. **Templates for Mrs. Numsen's Rose II**

2¼" Outer Petals (cut seven).

1⅞" Inner Petals (cut six).

1⅜" Center (cut one, gather and stuff).

B. Two halves stitched together.

C. Turned right side out, running stitched.

Gathered at the base.

FIGURE 10-1. Mrs. Numsen's Rose II

B.

Fold in half.

A. **Templates for Mrs. Numsen's Rose III**

Outer Petal (Cut ten).

Inner Petal (Cut six).

A. Center Cut one; gather and stuff.

C. **Floribunda Rose Templates**

Row 5

Row 4

Row 3

Row 2

Row 1

C. Center (cut one, gather and stuff).

Each petal has a small cuff folded back on it.

The Floribunda is the fullest of all Mrs. Numsen's Rose Versions.

Cut five of each row's petals; cut one center.

FIGURE 10-2. Mrs. Numsen's Rose III

BERIBBONED BOUQUET

2. Cut these circles in half. Sew all the pairs of two halves together on the machine, taking a narrow ⅛" seam (Figure 10-1B).

3. Turn these half circles right side out. Gather each across the bottom (Figure 10-1C).

4. *The Rose's Center.* Instead of a stuffed center, one inner petal is rolled tightly for the center and tacked at its base to hold this shape. Hold this rolled center upside down to attach subsequent petals to it. Each petal is sewn through its gathered, raw-edged base to the ones before it.

5. Sew the inner petals on first. Raw edges together, make sure the base of each is even with the previous petal. Each subsequent petal is sewn to, and overlaps the one before a bit. Move from inner to outer petals until all thirteen are used. The base remains flat and easy to sew to your background block.

BERIBBONED BOUQUET

Mrs. Numsen's Rose III:
These are the yellow roses at the center of the "Beribboned Bouquet."

1. *To form the "puff" center:* Gather the center circle (Figure 10-2A) into a shallow cup shape. Stuff in a teaspoon of polyester fiber and pull the thread tighter. Stitch loosely across the filling to hold it in. Secure the thread.

2. *Making the petals:* Cut six inner and ten outer petals. Fold each petal in half (Figure 10-2B). Use a running stitch along the curved raw edges. Pull these stitches to gather the petal, then secure them. (I like to string my gathered petals together from small to large. This keeps them organized. I cut each one off as I need it.)

3. *Starting the rose:* Hold the puff center wrong side up and cup the first small petal around it, aligning the raw edges of the center and petal (see Lesson 8). Stitch the petal to the center. Add the second petal, beginning at the midpoint of the first, overlapping clockwise. The third petal will overlap the second at the midpoint to cup the center.

4. Make a second round with the remaining three small petals, overlapping each by one third and keeping all raw edges on the same plane.

5. Add the larger petals in two rounds of five each. Pin the beginning and the end of a petal to the puff, and take additional tucks to gather it tightly to the puff. As the cluster of petals around the puff gets bigger, whipstitch each petal to the five previous layers, pulling in tiny tucks as you sew. These extra gathers tighten the base and relax the petal lip so the rose opens and lies flatter.

6. *Finishing:* Push at the center a bit to refine its shape. Then turn cuffs back (away from the center) on certain petals and tack these

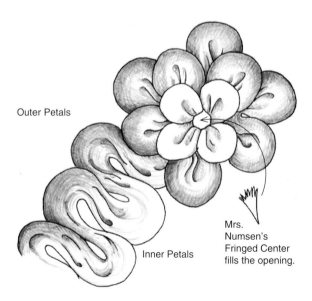

Outer Petals

Inner Petals

Mrs. Numsen's Fringed Center fills the opening.

FIGURE 10-3. The Center of a Ribbon Camellia

down if the fabric is too willful to hold the crease. Finally, tack the center down a bit with French knots from a single strand of cream-colored rayon Sulky embroidery floss.

The Floribunda Rose:

Sue Linker's Floribunda Rose is a large (3" diameter by ¾" deep) heavy rose. We give the templates here in Figure 10-2C. This stunning flower is constructed the same way as Mrs. Numsen's Rose III with two exceptions: Sue makes hers entirely of one variegated solid-color cotton and cuffs every petal.

Ruching a Ribbon Camelia:

While multiple ruching patterns make good flower petals, the zigzag (shell ruching taught in Lesson 9) pattern is particularly successful for small rounded petals. I used it on the primroses (at the far left center of my block) as well as on this camelia. Two more gathered-and-rolled flowers, this block's folded rose and the open rose are both taught in Lesson 1. For this camelia, begin with a yard of salmon-to-red 1"-wide shaded wire ribbon. Follow Figure 9-1, Ruched Flowers Made in Hand, steps A, B, and C, exactly. Because the ribbon is 1" wide, mark off every one inch. The outside petals are the red side of the ribbon, and the inside petals are the salmon side.

1. *To form the camelia's standing center:* Fold the strip from right to left so that the first salmon (inner) petal lies over the fourth salmon petal. Tuck the starting salmon "tail" under the first red (outer) petal (Figure 9-1). Tack-stitch the "valley" between the first red petal and the fifth red petal. Secure the stitches.

2. Flatten the five red petals in a wreath around the four salmon petals standing up in the center (Figure 10-3).

3. Twist the strip so that the fifth red outer petal completely covers the fifth salmon inner petal, which lies flat beneath it. (You'll probably see the potential for all sorts of five-petaled flowers at this point!)

4. Push the sixth red petal slightly to the left so that it shows underneath, between the first and the fifth red petal (Figure 10-3). The seventh red petal shows beneath the first and second red petal, and so forth. Surround the center by as many concentric rounds of red petals as you desire. Tack-stitch the center of each petal to the gathering line of the next row, which lies beneath it.

5. Cut off the extra ribbon when you judge the flower is big enough. Tuck the raw edge under the bloom. Fill the center with a yellow Mrs. Numsen's Fringed Center from Lesson 2 (See Figure 10-3 again).

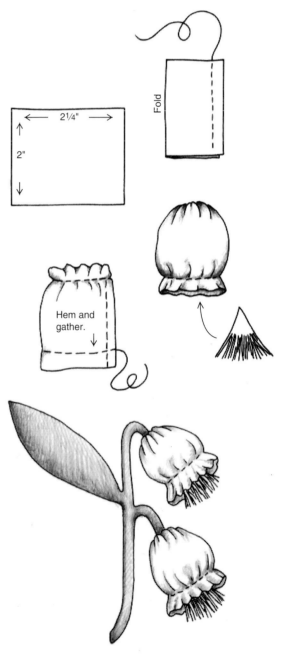

FIGURE 10-4. Foxgloves or Bluebells

Foxgloves or Bluebells:

This cupped flower can be a foxglove or a blue-bell, depending on the size (Figure 10-4). For the bluebell, cut a 2" length of 1"-wide ribbon. Blue-to-white ombré ribbon (wire removed) works well. (For the foxglove, cut a 2½" length of 1⅜"-wide ribbon.) Fold it in half, matching the cut edges, and seam ¼" from the raw edge. Gather the top edge tightly. Secure the stitches. Then gather ¼" from the lower edge and pull to nip the bell in slightly. Set the flower on the background with the exposed seam hidden underneath, and push it up slightly to hide the gathering of the top. Push ¼ teaspoon of polyester stuffing up into the cup of the flower, and appliqué the curved top of the cup to the background. Finish by tucking a Mrs. Numsen's fringed center into the lip so it peaks out a bit, and secure by stitching from underneath.

Bluebells From Cut Cloth:

1. Cut a 2" x 2¼" rectangle of blue cotton (Figure 10-4).

2. Fold the rectangle in half lengthwise. Sew the side seam in matching blue thread. Backstitch at the top of the seam.

3. Continuing with the same thread, take small running stitches across the top edge and pull to gather.

4. Fold a ½" hem inside, at the bottom. Sew ¼" above the fold, circling the "bell" with a running stitch. Pull these stitches to give the flower a "waist" and its finished shape. Put the vertical seam to the back, and push the top up and back to hide the gathered seam. Appliqué the upper half to the background and tuck in a fringe.

The Primroses:

Make a five-petaled flower shell-ruched out of ⅛"-wide satin ribbon. Place an upside-down "Lily of the Valley" in the center.

Lilies of the Valley:

Stick a ¾" adhesive dot on the right side of tie-dyed blue-and-white fabric. Sew fine running stitches around the dot, then cut out the circle ⅛" beyond the stitching (Figure 10-5). Remove the dot and pull the gathering thread tight to form a little bell. Secure the thread and ruffle the raw

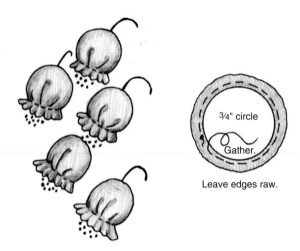

FIGURE 10-5. Lily of the Valley

edge. Then push the flower up against the background a bit to expose its center, and appliqué just the upper third of it to the background. For detail, ink in tiny stems between the clustered bells.

Puff-Centered Peony Bud:

1. Cut one 1¾"-diameter circle of silk for the center. Do a running stitch ⅛" inside the raw edge around this circle. Gather the stitches loosely to cup the fabric. Stuff with a level tablespoonful of polyester fiber and pull the gathers to form a tight round bud center. Secure the stitches.

2. Cut three 1⅜"-diameter circles of silk satin. Fold each in half on the bias and gather ⅛" inside the rounded raw edge. Cup these around the center, overlapping each petal by ¼" (Figure 10-6A).

3. Cut three 1¾"-diameter circles. Gather as before (step #2) and outline the bud and its tight inner petals with a round of three more, just barely overlapping, petals (Figure 10-6B). The base of the peony bud is all on one level.

Inked detail:

Scale is a consideration in any needle art. Inkwork can be done on a finer scale, even, than fine embroidery. In my "Beribboned Bouquet," pen and ink were used for some of the flower stamens, the moss on the rosebuds, and the veins on the angular leaves made from solid-color tie-dyed fabric. The Pigma SDK .01 pen was used in both black and brown. Iron-set after inking.

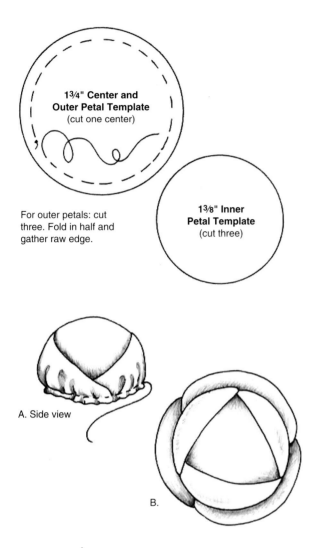

FIGURE 10-6. Puff-Centered Peony Bud

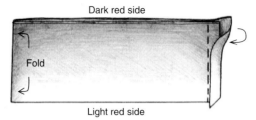

A. 1½" x 5" ribbon, folded in half and seamed.

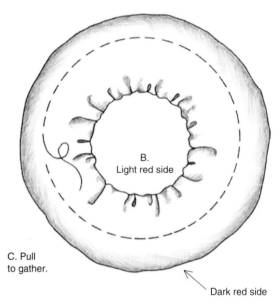

The light red side becomes the outside of the flower.

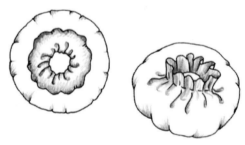

The finished posy can look like either of these.

FIGURE 10-7. Red Wire-Ribbon Posies

Red Wire-Ribbon Posies:

1. Cut a 5" strip of 1½"-wide shaded (light to dark red) wire ribbon. Seam its ends together. Make one seam ½" wide (¼" wider than the other) so that you can fold it to encase and finish the ¼" seam (Figure 10-7A).

2. Gather the light-colored side to a circle 1" in diameter (Figure 10-7B).

3. Run a line of gathering stitches ⅓" in from the dark-colored side (Figure 10-7C). Pull to gather, leaving a ¼"-diameter circle at the flower's center.

4. Pin the flower so that its inner "lips" sit at the center or just above center. Appliqué the base to the background fabric.

Christmas Cactus Bud:

This construction follows that of the inner Peony bud in Figure 10-6. Start with a 2" *crêpe de Chine* circle. Softly gather the circumference ⅛" in from edge. Stuff with a full teaspoon of batting. Pull the gathering thread tightly. Cut two more 2" circles in ombré ribbon for the petals that overlap the bud. Fold each in half so the color change is perpendicular to the fold and gather along the curved edge. Gather a bit, fit to bud, and pull gathers up. Then stitch to bud edge. Repeat for other side. Appliqué to block, then appliqué a calyx (cut of Ultrasuede®) to cap it.

A Symbolic Bouquet

A harkening back to the Language of Flowers introduced our lessons. Let's end them here, then, with a reading, insofar as it can be done, of this Beribboned Bouquet. The meanings are those given in my book, *Spoken Without a Word, A Lexicon of Selected Symbols*:

- *Red Chrysanthemum:* "I love you." Chinese Chrysanthemum: "Cheerfulness under adversity."

- *Rose (single):* Simplicity.

  Rose, fullblown: "I love you."

  Rose, musk: American beauty, charming.

  Damask Rose: "Brilliant complexion, Ambassador of Love."

  China Rose: Ever fresh beauty.

- *Bluebell:* Delicacy, constancy.

- *Foxgloves:* (No meaning given, but perhaps these are Cowslips, which mean "Winning grace.")

- *Lily of the Valley:* Sweetness, renewed happiness, Spring, Birth of Christ, Immortality, Tears of the Virgin Mary, Symbol of Motherhood, "Let us make up!"

- *Rosebuds:* Beauty, purity, youth (Moss Rosebud: "I confess my love.")

- *Christmas Cactus:* (No meaning given.)

- *Primroses* (five-petaled posies): Early youth, young love.

- *Crown of Roses:* A symbol of superior merit (Garland of Roses means "Virtue's Reward.")

- *Red Camelia:* Unpretentious excellence.

And, like the bouquet presented to the Diva, applauding her moving performance, this bouquet is for you, dear reader, at lessons' end.

Part Three: The Patterns

The patterns for 39 blocks are given on the following pages and on the pullout sheet after page 176. The 33 block patterns are given on one, two, and four pages. The pattern transfer method for block designs depends on the number of pages as explained in "Part One: Getting Started" in *Volume 1*. Whenever possible, patterns are presented on the outside corner of the page for easier tracing. The five border patterns on the pullout sheet after page 176 may be used with the medallion on that sheet or with any grouping of individual blocks.

FERNS AND FLORIBUNDA ROSES, the center of an original-design wall quilt by Sue Linker, 1992. No pattern given. (Photo: S. Linker)

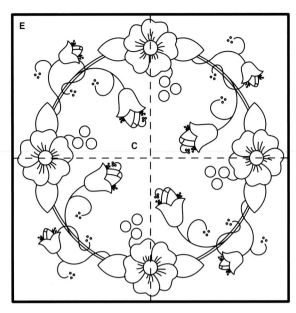

PATTERN #1: "Roses are Red"

Type: "Beyond"; Designed by Gwendolyn LeLacheur

To make this block, refer to Lessons 3, 7, and 8; in *Volume I,* Lessons 6 and 9.

This wreath has a relaxed, inviting look. Gwen LeLacheur who designed the pattern has used fabrics that make this block sing. She began with the superfine stem, then the leaves and large-petaled flowers. The embroidery in chain stitch, blanket stitch and French knots is all done in two strands of ginger-colored floss.

Key:

1. Superfine stems   2. Blanket-stitched leaves
3. Petaled flower in graduated shades
4. Folded Circle Roses (Use Template A for inner buds, B for outer buds.)   5. Embroidered details: Stem stitch and French knots
6. Stitched rose moss   7. Stem-stitched petal detail

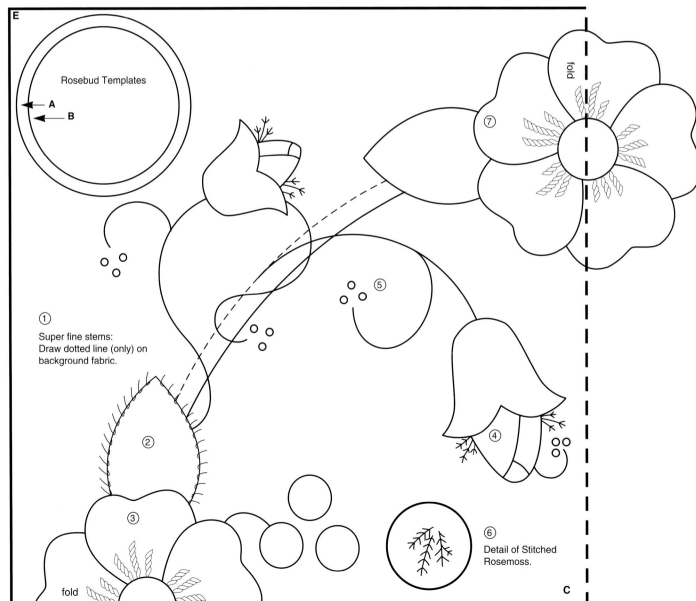

Rosebud Templates

A
B

① Super fine stems: Draw dotted line (only) on background fabric.

⑤

②

③

④

⑥ Detail of Stitched Rosemoss.

fold

fold

⑦

E

C

PATTERN #2: "I Promised You a Rose Garden"

Type: "Beyond"; Designed by Gwendolyn LeLacheur

To make this block, refer to Lesson 8; in *Volume I*, Lessons 9 and 10.

This lovely original's repetitive nature makes the design quickly graspable. But the texture of the multi-petaled roses and the swirl of the small (two strands floss) embroidered stems, keeps one fascinated. Mrs. Numsen's Rose I is featured in the eight large roses. Twelve folded rosebuds (1¾"-diameter circles in color #3) are supported by stem-stitched green stems and accented with red French knots. Begin by making a superfine stem from a ¾"-wide piece of bias. Make leaves with a freezer paper template on the inside. For the full-blown rose (Mrs. Numsen's Rose I), follow the directions in Lesson 8. Finish with the embroidery noted on the pattern.

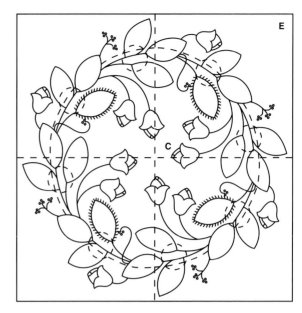

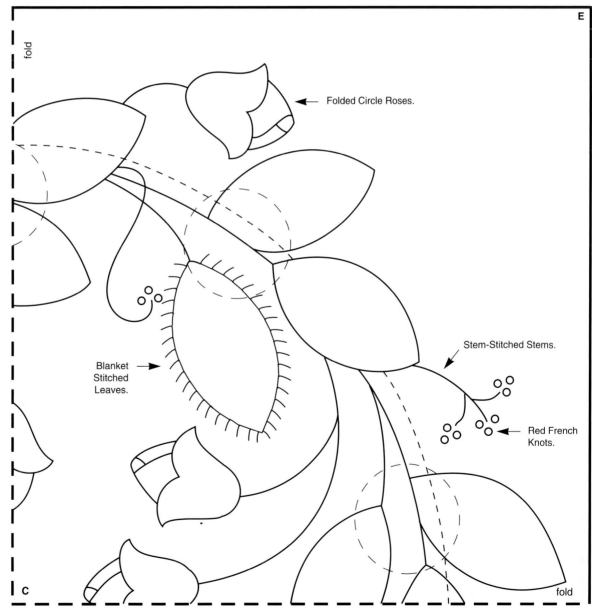

Folded Circle Roses.

Stem-Stitched Stems.

Blanket Stitched Leaves.

Red French Knots.

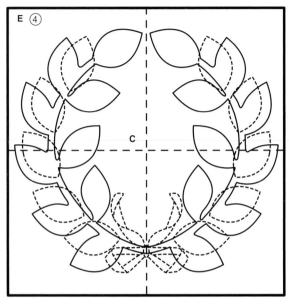

PATTERN #3: "Wreath of Folded Ribbon Roses"

Type: "Beyond"; Designed by the author

To make this block, refer to Lessons 5 and 7; in *Volume I,* Lessons 2 and 6.

This is a delightfully simple block, elegantly done in a carefully chosen green cloth. Choose a medium to large-scale print, which breaks the green up a bit and gives the impression of a bit more complexity than there actually is in the wreath's straightforward shape. P & B Textiles' *Baltimore Beauties* green "Ombré Leaves" is excellent for this block. The rosebuds, too, look more lifelike folded in shaded wire ribbon or mottled cloth. For the antique look, try combining P & B's *Baltimore Beauties* engraved Baltimore Rose pattern in its red, peach, and orange colorways.

PATTERN #3: "Wreath of Folded Ribbon Roses"

Second page

This strong, easy-to-construct block showcases a calligraphed inscription or an inked drawing at its center. *Baltimore Beauties and Beyond, Volume II* teaches you how to do this. Alternatively, elegant calligraphed sentiments border P & B's "Classic Album Cloth," and one of these, framed by a reverse appliquéd oval, would be this block's perfect finishing touch. *Baltimore Beauties Fabric Notes:* P & B Textiles invited my design consultation on a 38-piece fabric line named *Baltimore Beauties* in honor of this series. Our needs (both in replicating old Baltimore and in taking it beautifully beyond) helped determine that fabric's style. For this reason, *Baltimore Beauties Fabric Notes* are included, where possible, on subsequent patterns.

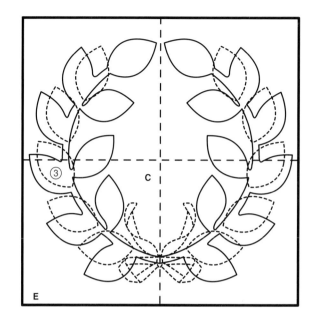

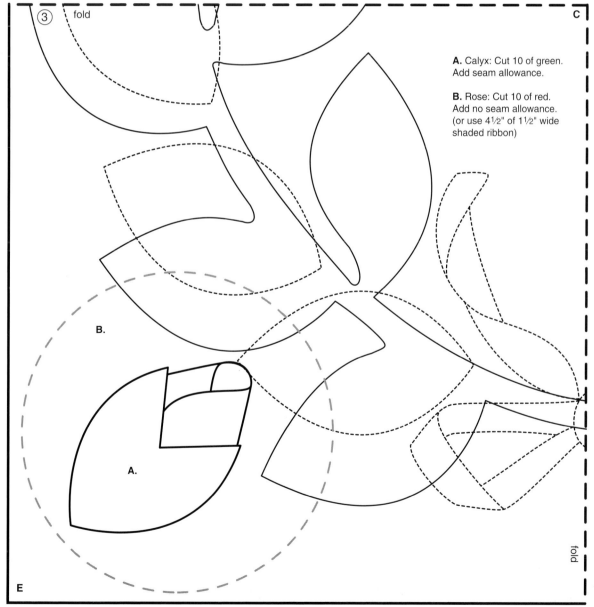

A. Calyx: Cut 10 of green. Add seam allowance.

B. Rose: Cut 10 of red. Add no seam allowance. (or use 4½" of 1½" wide shaded ribbon)

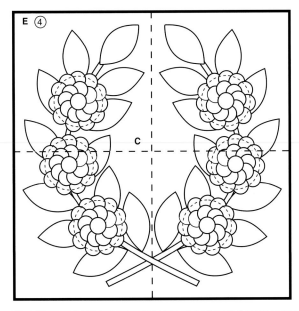

PATTERN #4: "Crown of Ten Penny Roses"

Type: "Beyond"; Designed by the author

To make this block, refer to Lessons 4 and 7; in *Volume I*, Lessons 9 and 10.

The ten-penny nomen derives from the dime-sized circle petals on these roses. This flower's basted-only antique original repeated twill-like Turkey red cotton petals. Debbie Ballard stitched this bloom in a plethora of red textures against a backdrop of dramatic green prints. The effect is dynamic! Office dots (³/₄" diameter) ease the stitching as Lesson 4 explains. For stem placement, draw only the dashed outer line of the stems on the background cloth. For flower placement, draw the six dotted circles.

Baltimore Beauties Fabric Notes: For the leaves, mix greens from these P & B designs: Ombré Leaves,

PATTERN #4: "Crown of Ten Penny Roses"

Second page

Ombré Ferns, Baltimore Rose, and Vermiculates. Two strips of the Ombré Leaves, cut on the bias, then seamed together to form chevrons, make ideal "split leaves." So does one strip of Ombré Leaves sewn (right or wrong side up) to a Vermiculate green.

For the Rose Petals, use the same patterns just listed, but in shades of Victoria Red or Baltimore Blue.

For the Background Cloth, use P & B's "Classic Album Cloth," which reproduces the words from Lesson 2 in *Baltimore Beauties and Beyond, Volume II*. Perhaps one of these is the perfect finishing touch for this block's center.

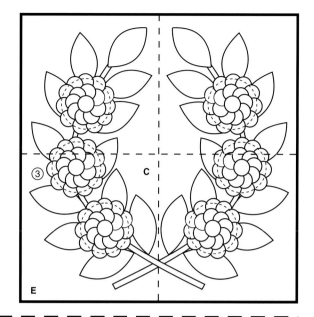

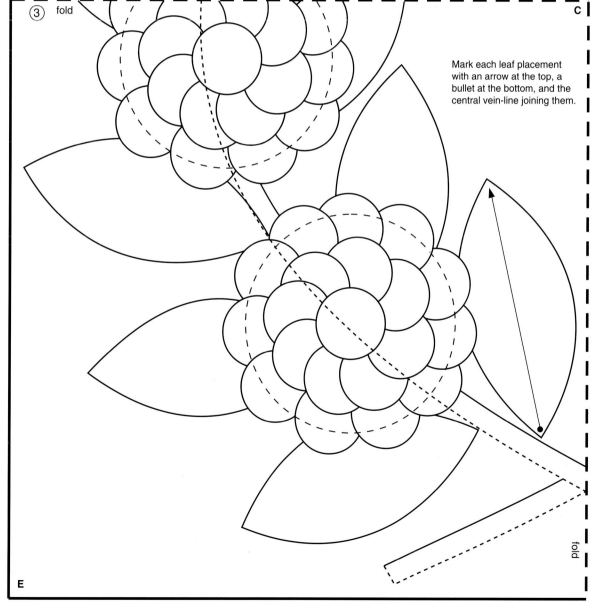

③ fold

Mark each leaf placement with an arrow at the top, a bullet at the bottom, and the central vein-line joining them.

C

fold

E

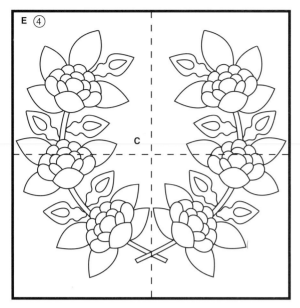

PATTERN #5: "Crown of Quilted Roses"

Type: "Beyond"; Designed by the author

To make this block, refer to Lesson 7; in *Volume I*, Lessons 9 and 10.

Here, rich red *crêpe de Chine* silk echoes the velvety depth of real roses. This style of stuffed-rose block was typically made in a simple two fabric red/green palette. Marjo Hodges quilted, then outlined each bud and each rose, petals and all, with the stem-stitch (or the outline stitch) done in silk buttonhole twist. If you backstitch-quilt the rose, you will be both quilting and embroidering it at the same time. Echoing the botanical authenticity seen in some antebellum Album blocks, Marjo embroidered the greenery with soft loden green floss twined with a beige thread. She's come delightfully close to the look of a real rose thorn streaked with red or beige.

"Part 3: The Patterns" continues on page 97 following the Color Section.

Mark each leaf with a placement arrow and bullet.

A. Detail: Leaf Embroidery.

The Color Section

1. FANCY FLOWERS BOUTIQUE FROM LESSON 1.

2. LESSON 1 INTRODUCES JUST A FEW OF THE BEAUTIES YOU'LL BE ABLE TO MAKE FROM THIS BOOK: Faye Labanaris' seamed and turned friendship rose (Lessons 1 and 5) is pictured here in its silverplate frame. Beside it, the author's ribbon rose looks old and fragile on its necklace setting. Who would guess that more such roses can be made up in just minutes? Nearby, an enticing selection of findings sits ready for floral adornment.

3. Lesson 2: VICTORIAN RIBBON BASKET WITH ROLLED WIRE RIBBON ROSES (Pattern #13). Designed and made by the author. (Photo: B. Hunt)

1

2

3

4

5

6

7

4. Lesson 4: BASKET OF QUARTER ROSES AND BUDS (Pattern #11). Designed and made by Melody Bollay. (Photo: S. Risedorph)

5. Lesson 4: APPLES IN THE LATE AFTERNOON (Pattern #15). Designed and made by the author. (Photo: B. Hunt)

6. Lesson 4: IVY BASKET WITH BOW (Pattern #16). Designed and made by Irene Keating. (Photo: S. Risedorph)

7. Lesson 2: BLESSINGS OF AUTUMN (Victorian Weave Basket Pattern #25). Designed and made by Carol Spalding. (Photo: S. Risedorph)

8

9

10

11

8. Lesson 2: RIBBONWORK BASKET FOR BRODERIE PERSE BLOOMS (Pattern #32). Designed by the author. Stitched by the author and Yvonne Von Nieda. (Photo S. Risedorph)

9. Lesson 4: FOLK ART BASKET OF FLOWERS (Pattern #14). Stitched by Wendy Grande. (Photo S. Risedorph)

10. Lesson 6: HOME GROWN BOUQUET (The basket is Pattern #41 in Baltimore Album Quilts). Designed by Elizabeth Anne Taylor. (Photo: S. Risedorph)

Note the yellow foundation, rather than the alternate yellow ribs of the antique original. Elizabeth drafted the flowers, many from Australia.

11. Lesson 6: FLOWERS FROM HOME (The basket is Pattern #40 in Baltimore Album Quilts). Designed and made by Roslyn Hay. (Photo S. Risedorph)

The exquisite realism of these flowers is augmented by fine botanical detail stitched in sewing thread or single-strand floss embroidery.

12

13

14

15

12. Lesson 6: TEXAS FINERY: BASKET SCULPTURE (Based on Pattern #41 in *Baltimore Album Quilts)*. Designed and made by Lisa DeBee Schiller. (Photo S. Risedorph)

There are Victorian Baskets seen on two planes at once in a sort of folk art perspective. So, too, one can "see" down into this basket, which is otherwise seen from the side.

13. Lesson 4: UNADORNED VICTORIAN BASKET OF FLOWERS (Pattern #12). Designed and made by Marsha Carter. (Photo: S. Risedorph)

14. Lesson 6: TEXAS TREASURES (Pattern #23). Designed and made by J. Jane Mc. Mitchell. (Photo: B. Hunt)

15. Lesson 7: FLOWER-WREATHED HEART (Adapation of Pattern #8). Bonnie Clifton Knezo. (Photo: S. Risedorph)

16

17

18

19

16. Lesson 7: FLOWER-WREATHED HEART WITH PANSIES (Adaptation of Pattern #8). Designed and made by Yolanda Tovar. (Photo: Y. Tovar)

17. Lesson 5: WILANNA'S BASKET GARDEN (Pattern #20). Designed and made by Wilanna Bristow. (Photo: S. Risedorph)

18. Lesson 7: CROWN OF QUILTED CHINTZ ROSES (Adaptation of Pattern #5). Made by Gladys Clayson. (Photo: S. Risedorph)

19. Lesson 7: CROWN OF TEN PENNY ROSES (Pattern #4). Designed and made by Debra L. Ballard. (Photo: B. Hunt)

20

21

22

20. Lesson 7: CROWN OF QUILTED ROSES (Pattern #5). Made by Marjo Hodges. (Photo: S. Risedorph)

21. Lesson 7: WREATH OF FOLDED RIBBON ROSES (Pattern #3). Designed by the author and made by Faye Labanaris. (Photo: B. Hunt)

22. Lesson 7: WREATH OF STUFFED ROSES (Pattern #20 in *Baltimore Album Quilts)*. Made by Marjorie Kruty. (Photo: S. Risedorph)

23

24

25

23. Lesson 10: NUMSEN BOUQUET II: BERIBBONED BOUQUET
(Pattern #22). Interpreted by Elly Sienkiewicz. (Photo: S. Kahn)

24. Lesson 10: NUMSEN BOUQUET III: NUMSEN FAMILY BOUQUET
REVISITED (Pattern #22). Interpreted by Nancy Hornback.
(Photo: S. Risedorph)

25. CELIA'S GARDEN, wall quilt (No pattern given). Designed
and made as a class teaching model by Faye Labanaris.
Approximately 22" x 22". (Photo: F. Labanaris)

26

27

28

26. Lesson 7: CROWN OF RUCHED ROSES (Pattern #6).
Designed and made by the author. (Photo: S. Kahn)

27. Lesson 5: JEANNIE'S BLUE BALTIMORE BASKET (Jeannie
Austin's basket, Pattern #19). Designed and made by Sue
Linker. (Photo: S. Risedorph)

28. Lesson 5: REGAL BIRD AMIDST THE ROSES (Pattern #18.
Raenell Doyle's basket, Jeannie's design). Designed and
made by Jeannie Austin. (Photo S. Risedorph)

29

30

31

32

29. Lesson 8: TOKEN OF GRATITUDE (Pattern #17 in *Volume I*). Cleda J. Dawson. (Photo S. Risedorph)

30. Lesson 5: JEANNIE'S BLUE BALTIMORE BASKET (Pattern #19). Designed by Jeannie Austin and made by Sue Linker. (Photo: S. Risedorph)

31. Lesson 5: JEANNIE'S IRIS, PANSY, AND PLEATED FLOWERS BASKET (Pattern #17. Raenell Doyle's basket, Jeannie's design). Made by Sue Linker. (Photo S. Risedorph)

32. Lesson 9: FANCY FLOWERS (Pattern #24A). Designed and made by the author. (Photo: S. Kahn)

33

34

35

36

37

33. Lesson 8: BALTIMORE BOUQUET (Pattern #21). Designed and made by Gwendolyn S. LeLacheur. (Photo: S. Risedorph)

34. Lesson 8: I PROMISED YOU A ROSE GARDEN (Pattern #2). Designed and made by Gwendolyn S. LeLacheur. (Photo: S. Risedorph)

35. Lesson 9: VASE OF FULL-BLOWN ROSES I (Pattern #10). Adaptation of a traditional design by Heidi Chesley Sandberg. (Photo: S. Risedorph)

36. Lesson 8: ROSES ARE RED (Pattern #1). Designed and made by Gwendolyn S. LeLacheur. (Photo: S. Risedorph)

37. Lesson 8: RICK RACK ROSES (Pattern #7). Designed and made by Gwendolyn S. LeLacheur. (Photo: S. Risedorph)

Detail of Quilt #1

Detail of Quilt #1

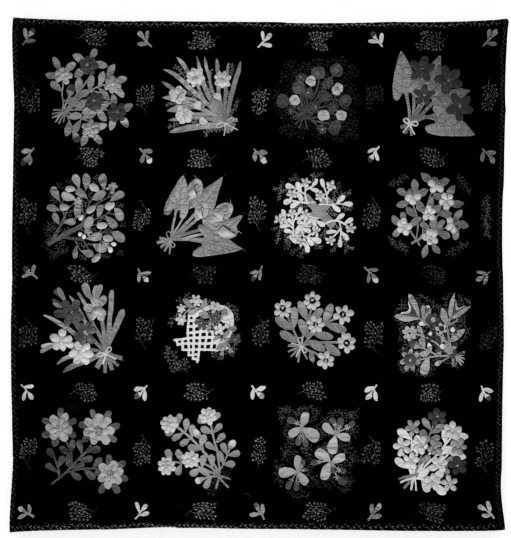

Quilt #1: ALBUM NO. 125, circa 1880-1900, 87½" x 88", probably Eastern Pennsylvania. (Photo: Collection of Ardis and Robert James)

Silk and satin; appliquéd, pieced, and embroidered. This exquisite example of Victorian needlework is rare, intricate, and detailed. The indication of a third dimension in the blooms, especially the calla lilies, is superb.

Detail: Quilt #2 (Annie's blooms made with Clotilde's Perfect Pleater®)

Detail: Quilt #2 (The eagle's wing feathers are formed by folded circles.)

Quilt #2: BLUE ALBUM, designed and made by Annie Tuley, 1991, 87" x 87". (Photo: Gary Bankhead Photography) Machine appliquéd and machine quilted. Annie has taken the Baltimore-style Album to the brink of yet another century with her computerized sewing machine.

Detail: Quilt #3

Detail: Quilt #3

Quilt #3: A TOKEN OF REMEMBRANCE (For pattern, see Sources), made by Jenifer Buechel, 1992, approximately 40" x 40". (Photo S. Risedorph)

Cotton prints, lamé, hand-dyed silk, lace, and beading.

This exquisite nouvelle Victorian quilt is an original design with hand-painted and calligraphed cloth. A number of fancywork techniques such as stuffed work, reverse appliqué, and beading enhance its beauty.

Quilt #4: SMITHSONIAN BASKET ALBUM QUILT, 94" x 104" including fringe. (Photo: Smithsonian Institution)

Silk top, including velvet, lined with cotton muslin; cotton fiber padding under appliqué; silk embroidery. Silk lining. No filling. Donated to the Smithsonian in 1933 by Mary Jane Moran's daughter, who reported that her mother (Mary Jane Green) had made this quilt as a bride of 18 in Baltimore, Maryland. Mary Jane wed John J. Moran on March 2, 1846.

Quilt #5: FANCY FLOWERS WALL HANGING (Adaptation of Lesson 9's Pattern #24 into a bordered wall quilt), made by Faye Labanaris, approximately 20" x 20". (Photo: F. Labanaris).

Faye's quilt has been lost, stolen, or it has strayed. Any information regarding this quilt would be greatly appreciated.

Quilt #6: Album Quilt. circa 1850, 80¾" x 68¾". (Photo: Abby Aldrich Rockefeller Folk Art Center, Williamsburg, Virginia)

Varied cottons with some silk details. "The quilt is inscribed 'To Emma' and a wee bird calls, 'Louise Present' (possibly meaning 'Louise's Present') but no other identifications are known." Wonderfully realistic flora include fuchsia, bleeding heart, and geranium plants. The Lord's Prayer is inscribed in the central wreath (Pattern #34 in the pullout section after page 176).

Quilt #5

Wreath Center Detail: Quilt #6 (Pattern #34)

Quilt #6

Quilt #7: KAY'S QUILT OF BALTIMORE BLOOMS, designed and made by Faye Labanaris, 1992. Approximately 50" x 50". (Photo: F. Labanaris)

This gem raises the stature of a four block Album to masterpiece heights. With exquisite dimensional details and impeccable design, Faye has truly created an heirloom. And she made it just within nine months for her Kay, the "baby doctor."

PATTERN #5: "Crown of Quilted Roses"

Second page

The original straight-stitching on buds and leaves would likely have been done in wool. One also sees closely worked patches of straight-stitched silk highlights on the plump round of the petals. The wool straight stitches may have been related to the concurrent Victorian fad of Berlin Work, a sort of needlepoint done in tapestry yarn. *Pattern transfer suggestion for any crown or wreath with vertically symmetrical leaves:* Make a complete (two-tipped) freezer paper leaf pattern, but snip the bottom end blunt for easy removal of the template. This allows you to mass produce the leaves all in one size and shape, but still place them at different depths guided by your placement arrows and bullets. On designs where you want to vary the leaf fabrics, it means that you can make up lots of leaves, then play with their arrangement on the block.

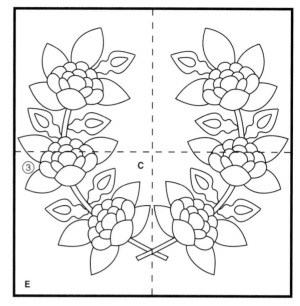

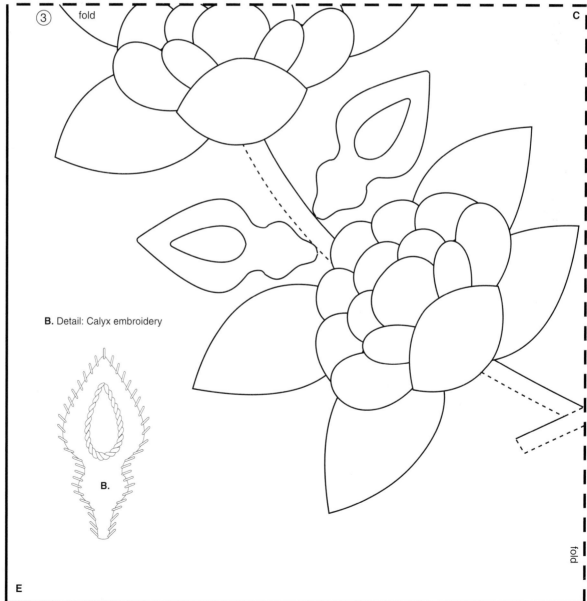

B. Detail: Calyx embroidery

B.

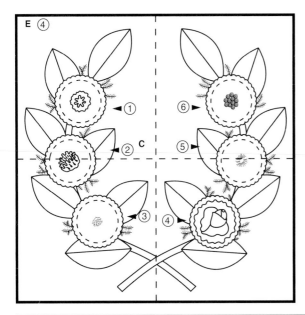

PATTERN #6: "Crown of Ruched Roses"

Type: "Beyond"; Designed by the author

To make this block, refer to Lesson 7; in *Volume 1*, Lessons 9 and 10.

This pattern was inspired by the picture of a circa 1852 Album Quilt made for Miss Isabella Battee and now owned by the Baltimore Museum of Art. I've combined that block's crown of ruched roses with the yellow-centered ruched roses from another Album. Lesson 7 teaches all the delights of this pattern from two-toned, embroidered leaves, to changing colors within a rose and giving each rose a different center. This is a fancywork block to linger over and enjoy! The key on the facing page tells which center was used on each rose, reading the roses counterclockwise from the top left.

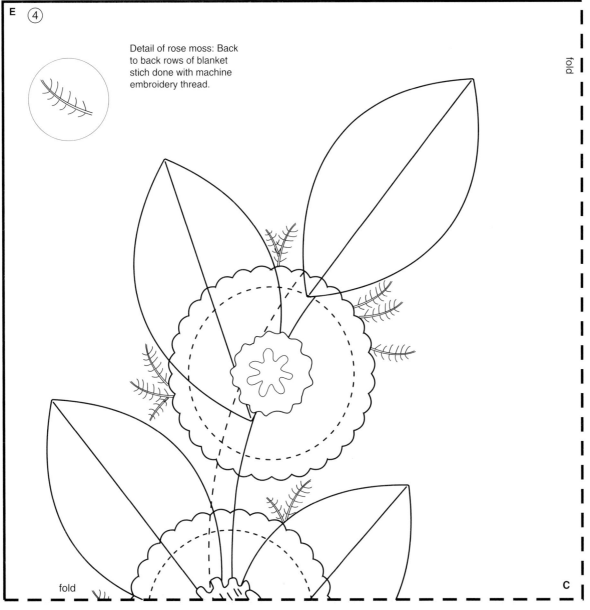

Detail of rose moss: Back to back rows of blanket stich done with machine embroidery thread.

fold

PATTERN #6: "Crown of Ruched Roses"

Second page

Key to the Ruched Roses' Novelty Centers:

Blossom #1: Mrs. Numsen's Fringed Center (gold China Silk) tucked into a Yo-Yo Center (hand-dyed silk)

Blossom #2: Yo-Yo Center

Blossom #3: Turkeywork (wool yarn, looped, then shorn off flat)

Blossom #4: Ruched Rose base topped by a Rolled Rose made by Method #2 (see Lesson 1).

Blossom #5: Mrs. Numsen's Fringed Center (corn-silk colored cotton).

Blossom #6: French Knot Center

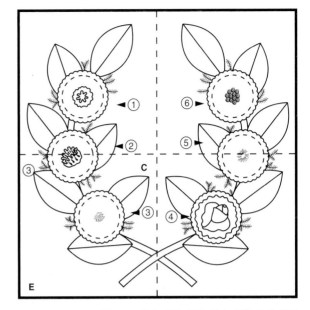

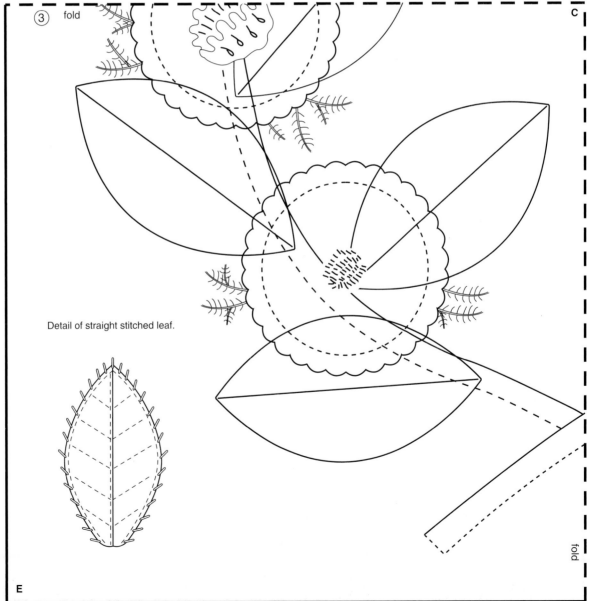

Detail of straight stitched leaf.

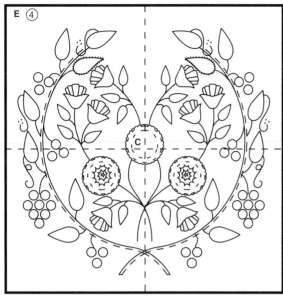

PATTERN #7: "Rick Rack Roses"

Type: "Beyond"; Designed by Gwendolyn LeLacheur

To make this block, refer to Lessons 7 and 8; in *Volume I*, Lessons 2 and 9.

This charming block combines several dimensional flowers. It is fancy needlework approached in an easy straightforward way. Lovely to look at and fun to make!

Gwen outlines her approach to this block:

1. Superfine Stems: Draw outer line only on fabric.
2. Leaves appliquéd, then outlined in buttonhole stitch (two strands of embroidery floss).
3. Grapes: Freezer paper (or ½" office dot) template underneath.

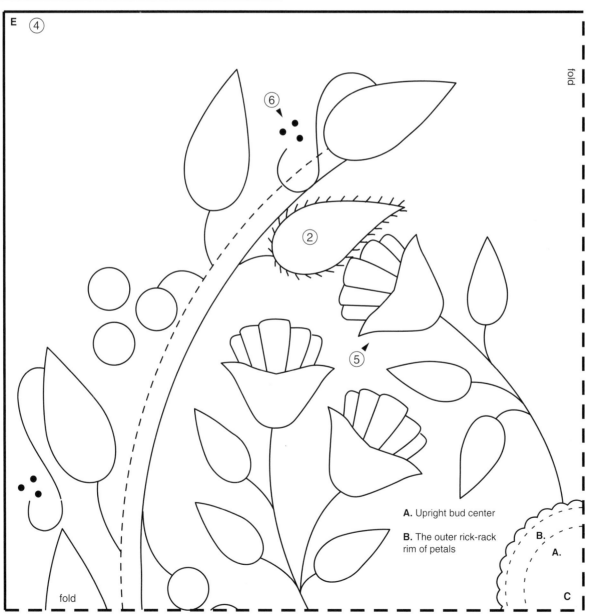

A. Upright bud center

B. The outer rick-rack rim of petals

PATTERN #7: "Rick Rack Roses"

Second page

Gwen's approach to this block continued:

4. Rick Rack Flowers: 1¼ yards of jumbo rick rack (instructions in Lesson 8).
5. Pleated Flowers: (instructions in Lesson 8).
6. Stems and French Knots: Embroider using two strands of embroidery floss.

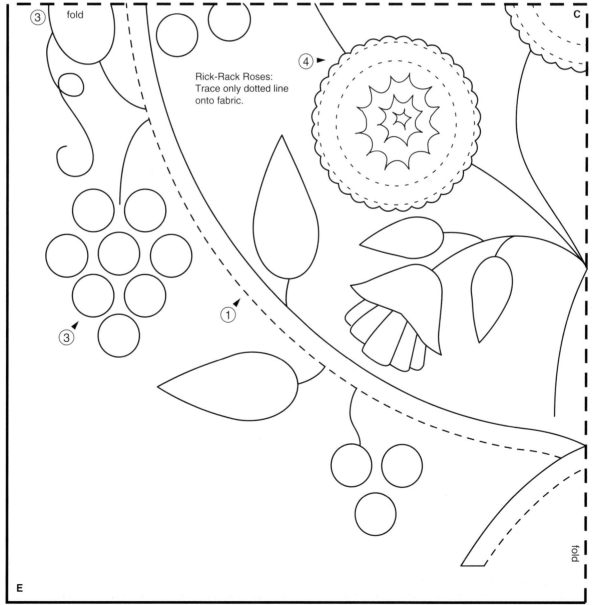

Rick-Rack Roses:
Trace only dotted line
onto fabric.

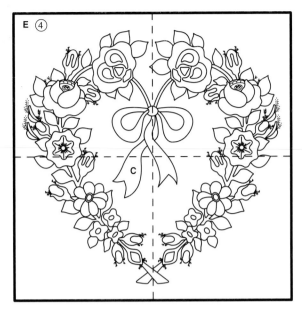

PATTERN #8: "Flower-Wreathed Heart II"

Type: "Baltimore-style"

To make this block, refer to Lesson 7; in *Volume 1*, Lessons 1, 2, and 5.

Early in the Baltimore Album Revival, this block began to be made. I had put a similar pattern in *Spoken Without A Word*, and it was one of the first of the ornate Victorian blocks to be reproduced by modern needlewomen. But few reproduced it exactly. The combination of the heart shape, so comfortably well-known to us, and the flowers we love to fashion, seemed to encourage people to make this sweet pattern very much their own. The pattern given here differs a bit from that in *Spoken Without a Word*. It offers several additional flowers to be included in your version. They come with the invitation to twine this bouquet just as it pleases you.

Alternate blossoms.

Join to lines below to complete bow tails.

fold

fold

PATTERN #8: "Flower-Wreathed Heart II"

Second page

In the Color Section, two lovely blocks in this style are pictured. One is by Yolanda Tovar (Color Plate #16) and the other by Bonnie Knezo (Color Plate #15). Yolanda added endearing pansies to her wreath long before they had become so popular again. And Bonnie had stitched her multi-petaled posies and turned them right side out with a delightful dimensionality years before so many of us also began to do this.

Baltimore Beauties Fabric Note: The Baltimore Blue Ombré Leaves fabric makes endearing versions of Lesson 2's pansies. Perhaps you'd like to tuck some of them into this wreath!

Alternate Leaf and Blossoms.

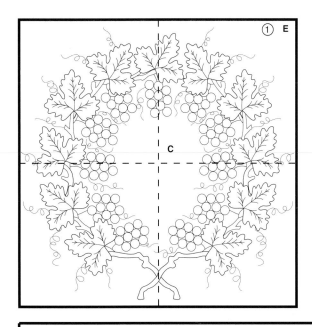

PATTERN #9: "Lovely Lane's Grapevine Wreath"

Type: classic "Baltimore"

To make this block, refer to Lesson 3; in *Volume I*, Lesson 9.

This lovely block is the cover photograph on *Baltimore Beauties and Beyond, Volume II*. You can see the original as the center block of Lovely Lane's antique Album in Photo 4-34 in *Volume II*. That block is a perfectly lovely piece of needle art. The leaves appear to be grape leaves cut from a print, then blanket or buttonhole stitched down, *broderie perse*-style. The small stuffed grapes are similarly shaded, their increasing intensities of hue giving a life-like depth to the clusters. The vine is not a simple stem, but seems also to have been cut from a print and embroidered down.

The leaf veins appear to have been printed or inked. The tendrils are chain stitched in one strand floss.

Flop pattern over to mark opposite side of wreath except top center bunch of grapes and leaf.

PATTERN #9: "Lovely Lane's Grapevine Wreath"

Second page

Tendrils in stitchery complete this block. Recognized long ago for its great beauty, this became a classic quilt's center block. One wonders if the whole appliqué (stem, leaves, fruit) were not perhaps cut from one piece of cloth and reconstructed on the Album block. For whatever reason, the original appears to be one block of a kind among the antique Albums, but it is already beginning to be repeated by us in our Revival Albums.

Baltimore Beauties Fabric Note: The richly shaded green of these grape leaves is echoed by the deep blue-green of P & B's Ombré Fern print. The print could also be pieced once, to imitate the leaves pictured on *Volume II's* cover. That print pattern also includes a colorway that, grape-like, shades from dove-gray to deep purple-blue.

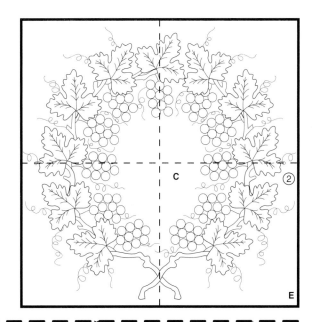

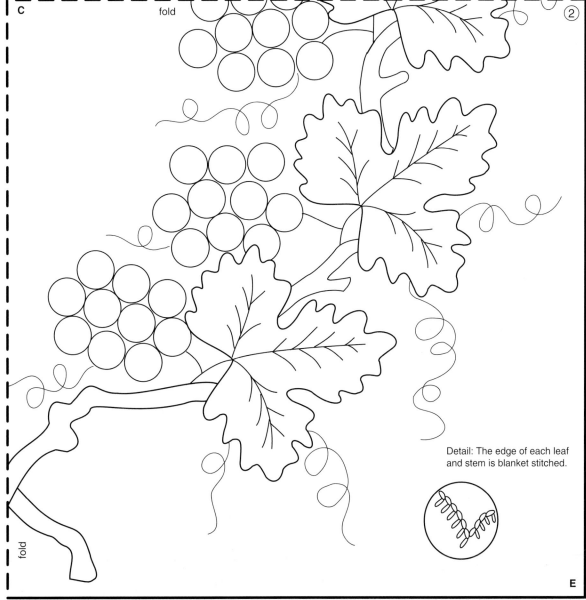

Detail: The edge of each leaf and stem is blanket stitched.

PATTERN #10: "Vase of Full-Blown Roses I"

Type: Baltimore-style

To make this block, refer to Lesson 9; in *Volume 1*, Lessons 2, 8, and 10.

This vase of roses (three red, one prominently white) is a common pattern—in some form—in the Baltimore-style Album Quilts. In one block that I've seen, there were five red roses, but, again, one prominently central white one. While I don't know why, I feel there must be some significance beyond aesthetics for the white rose's presence. These blocks could be very fancy as indeed we've seen, but this one is exceptionally simple, honing the style to its basics. The pattern you'll see is very straightforward. But Heidi Chesley Sandberg has interpreted the block so richly, using prints to advantage and ruching the overblown roses. This latitude of interpretation, from straightforward red, white, and green to rich prints and textures, has got to be part of Baltimore's appeal to so many of us.

PATTERN #10: "Vase of Full-Blown Roses I"

Type: Baltimore-style

Baltimore Beauties Fabric Note: For a rich, textured look, make these roses out of the Ombré Leaves print in Turkey Red, Russet, or Baltimore Blue with Victoria Green for foliage. To make the roses, follow Lesson 1's instructions for Rolled and Gathered Strip Flowers, Method #3. Cut the Ombré print 1¼" wide, on the bias, using pinking shears. For speed, machine stitch to gather in a line ⅛" parallel to the fold. When gathered, the shading in this "rainbow print" fabric is particularly dramatic. Mark your background cloth with a 1¾" circle for each rose. Coil the gathered strip, overlapping it slightly from a fringe at the center to the outside of the circle. The dimensional appearance of the Baltimore Blue Ombré Leaf stripe is perfect for giving contour to this simple compote shape. Such realism is the style taught us by old Baltimore.

PATTERN #11: "Basket of Quarter Roses and Buds"

Type: "Beyond"; Designed by Melody Bollay

To make this block, refer to Lesson 4; in *Volume I*, Lessons 5, 9, and 10.

A few years ago, a set of unfinished Album blocks was discovered, preserved in a drawer long warped shut in the Sands House, the oldest surviving wooden house in Annapolis, Maryland. Among the blocks was a basted bouquet with pleated flowers and a rose constructed of multiple, overlapped circle petals. These blooms were basted only, not yet sewn. Modern ones inspired by that rose have blossomed in several contemporary Albums. Sticky-paper circle templates simplify the construction, and Melody Bollay has given the rose a

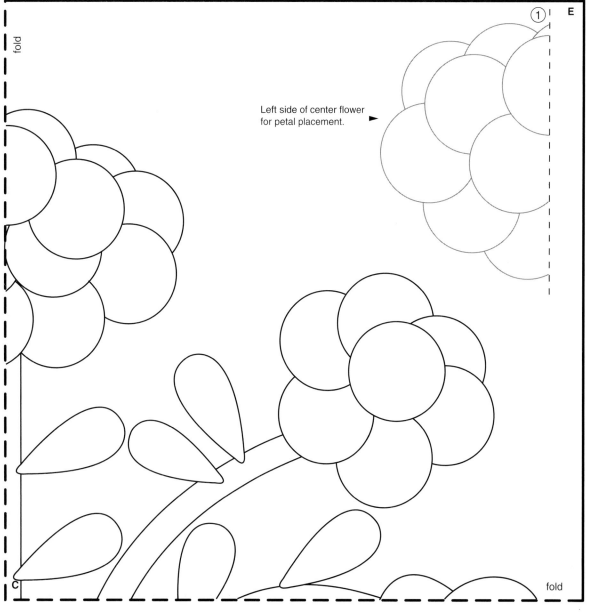

Left side of center flower for petal placement.

PATTERN #11: "Basket of Quarter Roses and Buds"

Second page

certain realistic perspective in this graphically easy block. The basket is even easier to make than the rose. The whole block is so appealing that it would enhance any Album.

Baltimore Beauties Fabric Note: To add a bit more realism to this simple basket, consider using one of the author's P & B design series' Basketweave prints. The basket could also be done over a monochromatic Vermiculate print foundation.

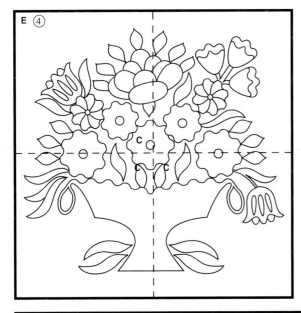

PATTERN #12: "Unadorned Victorian Basket of Flowers"

Type: classic "Baltimore"

To make this block, refer to Lesson 4; in *Volume I*, Lessons 5 and 10.

This design appears in the classic Album, inscribed "Ladies of Baltimore," Quilt #4 in *Baltimore Album Quilts—Historic Notes and Antique Patterns*. It is the simplest of baskets, one of those made from a single piece of cloth. But how cleverly and how clearly Victorian is its style! Even the flowers and the color scheme are simple. Yet the block itself fits beautifully into any Album, old or new. Learning from old Baltimore, Marsha Carter incorporates tie-dyes (ombré-like) to add a bit of depth to the flat shapes, and fools one's sense of time by adding an antique yellow calico.

PATTERN #12: "Unadorned Victorian Basket of Flowers"

Second page

Baltimore Beauties Fabric Note: Try the red Ombré Leaves stripe to make this basket; the look is exquisitely antiquarian! Then incorporate some of the simpler calico-like vermiculate prints (right and wrong sides up) in the flowers. Because the basket is so simple, why not fill it with a bouquet of your own design? Try a simple background of fused foliage: the Ombré Fern drapes gracefully while the Ombré Leaves stand up perkily. For naturalism and dimension, try double-fusing the ferns, leaving their fused edges raw, but sewing them to the background by running-stitching the veins.

Use this bloom in place of 'B' on right side.

PATTERN #13: "Victorian Ribbon Basket with Wire Ribbon Roses"

Type: "Beyond"; Designed by the author

To make this block, refer to Lesson 2; in *Volume I*, Lessons 5 and 10.

How can something so richly Victorian looking be so fast and simple? Lesson 2 explains. I designed this block as a 1½ hour Houston Quilt Market class to show shopowners how to use the wonderful ribbons so readily available today. (The block uses double-faced satin ribbon and shaded French wire ribbon.) We had fun. And based on that experience, I'd estimate that if you had your block "kit" all assembled, three hours would probably give you a fully prepared block all ready to sew. This block is not only easy, but its graphic strength

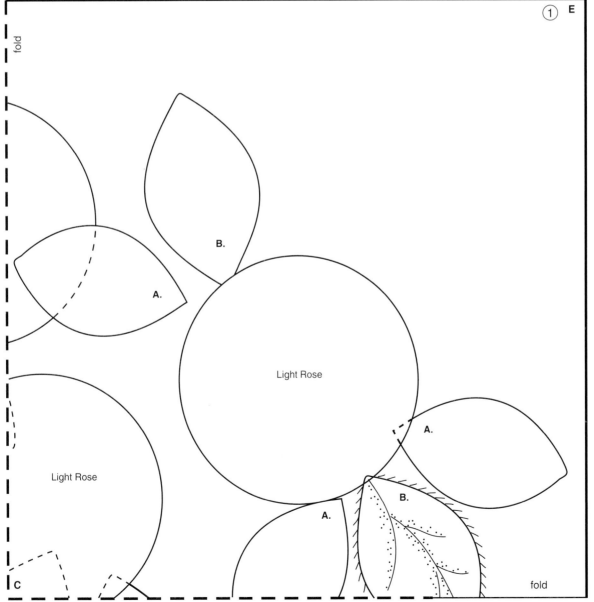

PATTERN #13: "Victorian Ribbon Basket with Wire Ribbon Roses"

Second page

makes it a wonderful home decor (pillow or framed picture) motif. If you assembled basted kits for several at once, each one would only take an evening to hand stitch into an exceptional gift.

Baltimore Beauties Fabric Note: Consider translating this ribbon block into cut cloth. I have made these roses with Lesson 1's Method #3: straight-tearing (intentionally fraying further) the gold Vermiculate and bias-cutting the red Ombré Leaves as described on Pattern #10. When you fold the strips wrong-side-in lengthwise, fold them ⅛" off-center to show a bit of the coloration of both the inside and the outside of the fabric. The Victoria Green Ombré Leaves print made into tucked leaves (Lesson 3) would enhance this block's bouquet.

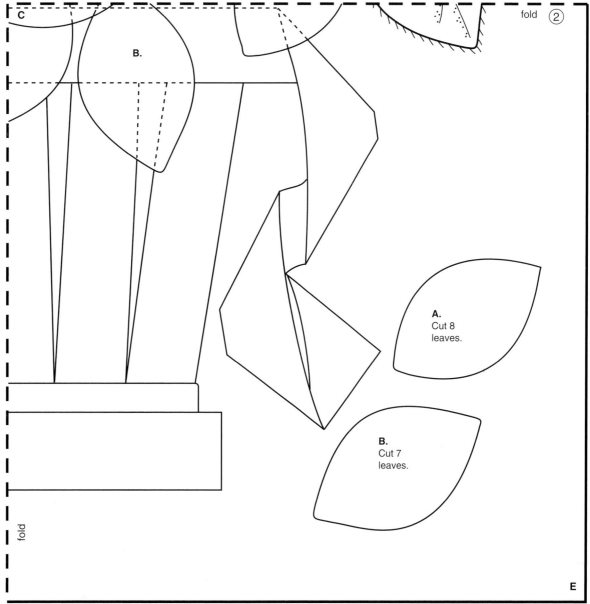

A.
Cut 8 leaves.

B.
Cut 7 leaves.

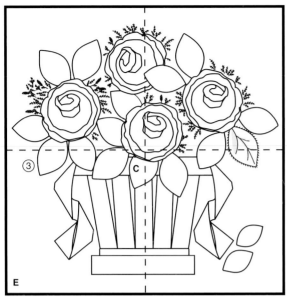

PATTERN #13: "Victorian Ribbon Basket with Wire Ribbon Roses"

Third page

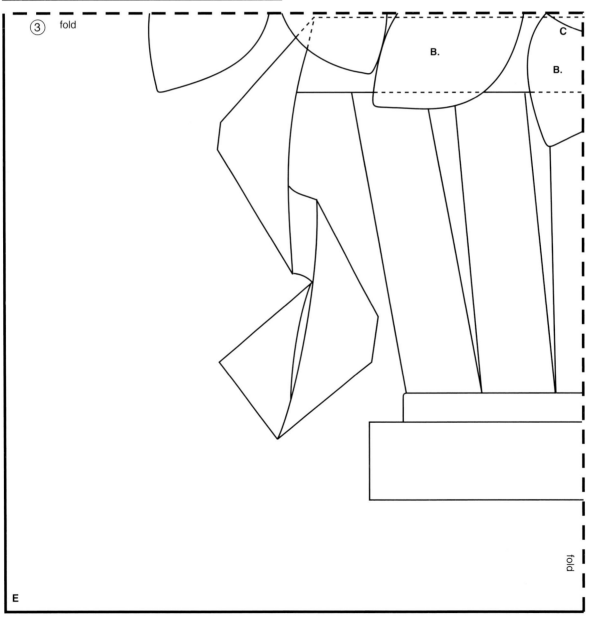

③ fold

B.

B.

C

fold

E

Pattern #13: "Victorian Ribbon Basket with Wire Ribbon Roses"

Fourth page

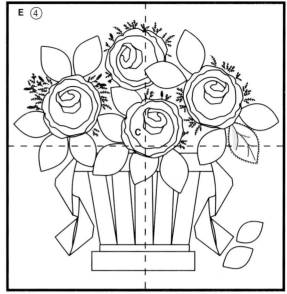

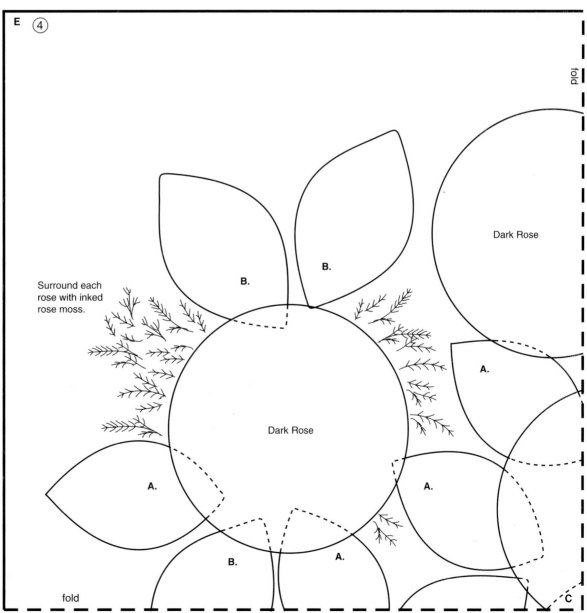

Surround each rose with inked rose moss.

Dark Rose

Dark Rose

B.

B.

A.

A.

A.

B.

A.

fold

fold

E ④

C

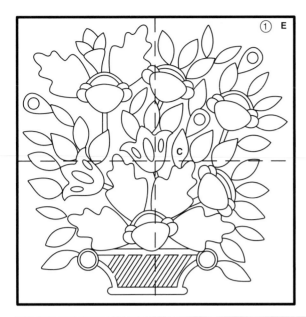

PATTERN #14: "Folk Art Basket of Flowers"

Type: classic "Baltimore"; from Quilt #3 in *Baltimore Album Quilts—Historic Notes and Antique Patterns*

To make this block, refer to Lesson 4; in *Volume I*, Lessons 5 and 10.

In the antique quilt, three blocks in a row echo a folk style that we tend to think of as Pennsylvania Dutch or "Deutsch" (which of course means Pennsylvania German). Great numbers of Germans had emigrated to Baltimore by the mid-19th century, and their influence in the Albums was noted by Dr. William Rush Dunton, Jr. The caricatured rose in this bouquet recurs repeatedly in red, yellow, and blue in these classic blocks. Over and over, one sees this color trio on linked cornucopias, baskets, stars, and flowers. Their combination seems significant.

PATTERN #14: "Folk Art Basket of Flowers"

Second page

The Odd Fellow and Rebekah's fraternal colors are now red, white, and blue. But their specific emblems (the three-linked chain and the five-pointed star-on-point) are always colored red, yellow, and blue in the classic Album Quilts. In those old quilts, yellow may have been substituted for white to preserve the secrecy so in vogue with those orders. Or perhaps they used yellow consistently to distinguish the symbol from the quilt's white background cloth. This basket's bouquet has a distinctively square profile. In their gravity-defying arrangement, the blooms imitate the stenciled balance of theorem paintings. Traditionally, then as now, we quiltmakers stitch eclectic folk arts of earlier times into our quilts.

PATTERN #14: "Folk Art Basket of Flowers"

Third page

In the original block, ombré rainbow prints are used throughout, adding that fabric's sophistication to the simplicity of the shapes. Here, Wendy Grande has interpreted the antique block with a fresh combination of fabrics echoing the rainbow prints with tie-dyes. The simple basket is worked on the palest yellow foundation, its ribs made of alternating fabrics. The easiest approach is to lay the foundation first, add the diagonal ribs, edge it, attach the base and brim, then the circular ornaments. Perhaps this folk-style quiltmaker's easy dismissal of botanical realism (many stems, for example, neither originate nor terminate in the basket) will convince you that whatever you do to these blocks is simply fine!

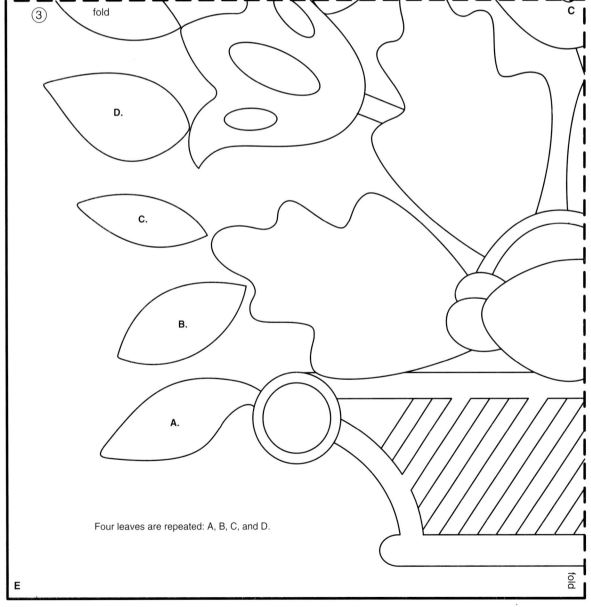

Four leaves are repeated: A, B, C, and D.

PATTERN #14: "Folk Art Basket of Flowers"

Fourth page

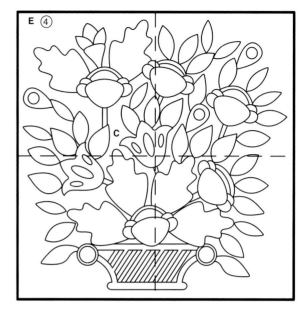

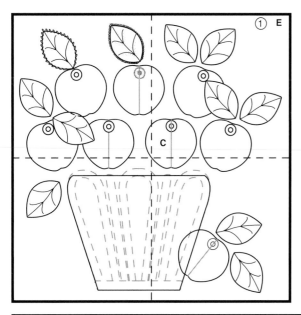

PATTERN #15: "Apples in the Late Afternoon"

Type: "Beyond"; Designed by the author

To make this block, refer to Lesson 4; in *Volume I*, Lesson 10.

The basket's tie-dyed fabric foundation gives this block the effect of mottled afternoon light. Hence its name. Some blocks sit at the back of your mind for a long time. Then, when you finally get down to making them, both the design and construction come quickly. This is such a block and its making marked a happy memory. The country inn inked in the lower lefthand corner commemorates the anniversary weekend there, when it was finished. (The inn's logo was transferred by the iron-on photocopy method described in *Baltimore Beauties and Beyond, Volume II*. It was then marked over with the same black Pigma .01 permanent pen used to embellish the block's leaf veins and apple stem-wells.) Hand-dyes were used for the appliqués. The

PATTERN #15: "Apples in the Late Afternoon"

Second page

ones that are two-toned have had one side appliquéd out of 1½"-wide shaded wire ribbon (with the wire removed). On the apples, the shaded ribbon overlay is stuffed. The basket is braided with ⅓"-wide raw-edged bias strips cut from a large print. [P & B's green Ombré Leaves would be perfect for this.] Double-sided basting tape aided the placement of these ribs. At the 1992 Empty Spools Seminar at Asilomar in California, Jan Dunn made a wonderful raw-edged-bias braided peck basket with its ribs and foundation both made of the same red print. She stenciled in her apples—and inspired my block. Thank you, Jan!

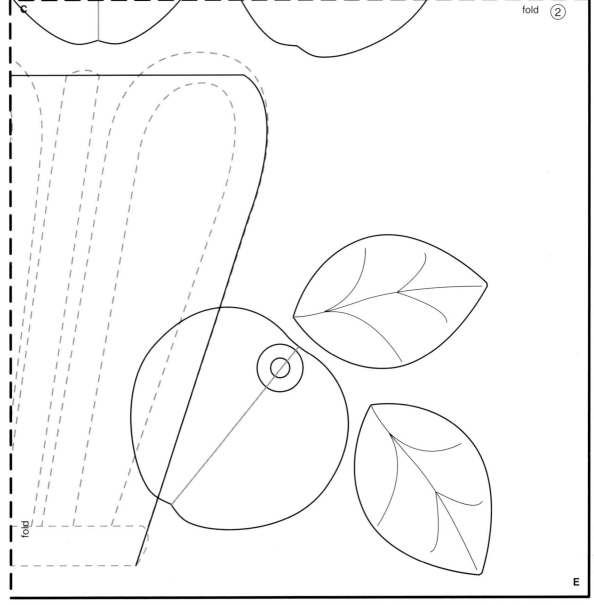

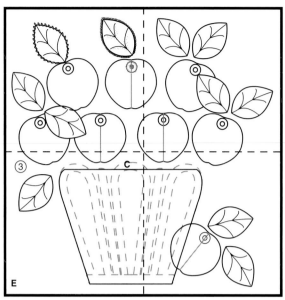

PATTERN #15: "Apples in the Late Afternoon"

Third page

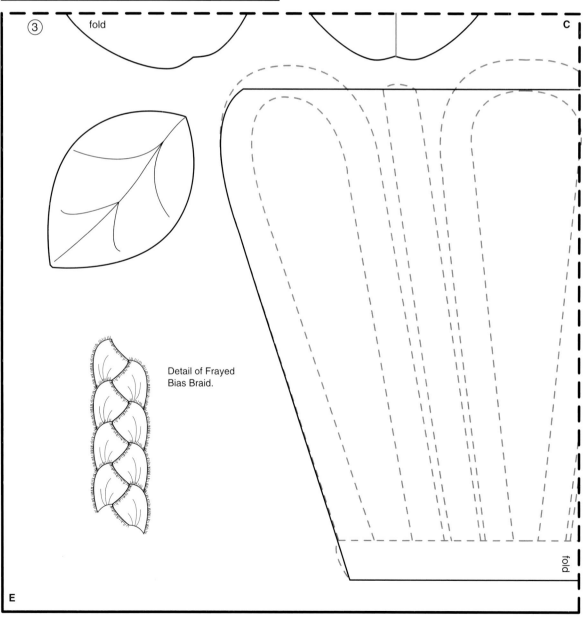

③

fold

C

Detail of Frayed
Bias Braid.

fold

E

PATTERN #15: "Apples in the Late Afternoon"

Fourth page

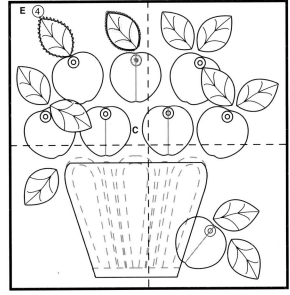

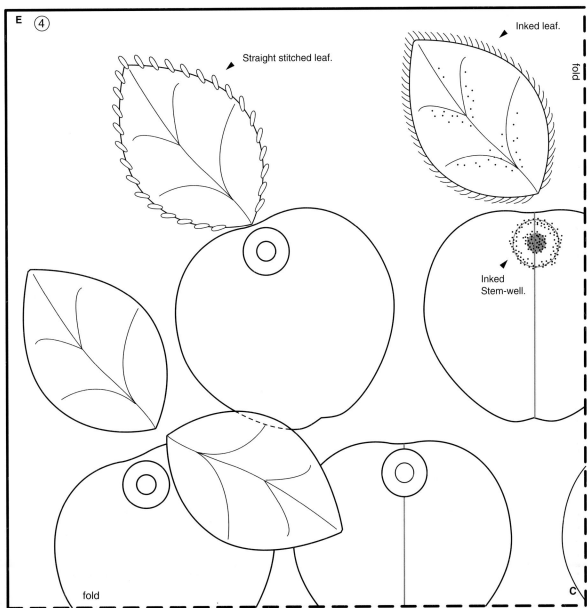

Straight stitched leaf.

Inked leaf.

fold

Inked
Stem-well.

fold

C

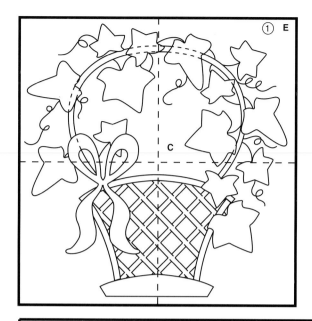

PATTERN #16: "Ivy Basket with Bow"

Type: "Beyond"; Designed by Irene Keating

To make this block, refer to Lesson 4; in *Volume I*, Lessons 1, 2, and 10.

A simple paper-folded basket shape, a graphic weave, and some pertly tied ivy (wound topiary-like around the handle) make this block both striking and unique. Irene sewed the basket's lattice pattern from one piece of cloth, by cut-away appliqué. Skill and patience are needed to sew all those sharp inside corners as beautifully as Irene has done. The same basket weave could more easily be done with pre-turned bias stems—layered, edged, and bracketed by base and brim. Irene brought photocopies of ivy leaves from her garden to this block's design session. She shares her charming stylization of those leaves here along with her basket pattern.

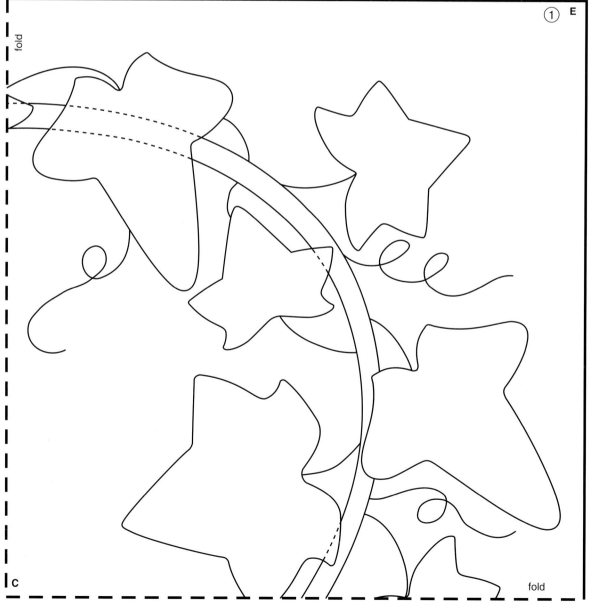

PATTERN #16: "Ivy Basket with Bow"

Second page

Baltimore Beauties Fabric Notes: Two of the mono-chromatic Vermiculate prints would combine well for this basket. Leaves cut from the "hand-dyed" Baltimore Rose print would make wonderful ivy foliage. This print has the richest, darkest greens, then soft-transitions into sunlit patches where the color lightens dramatically.

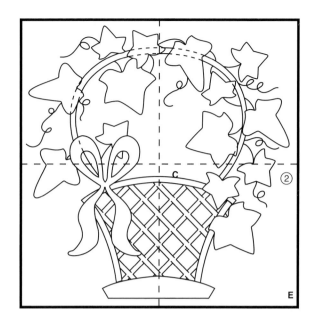

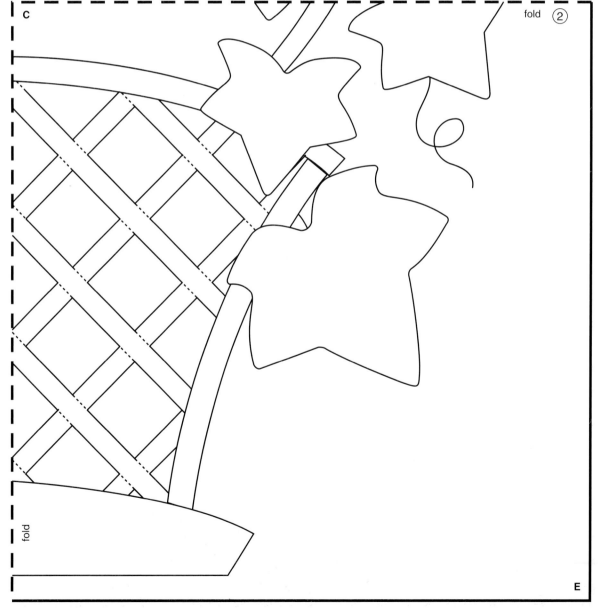

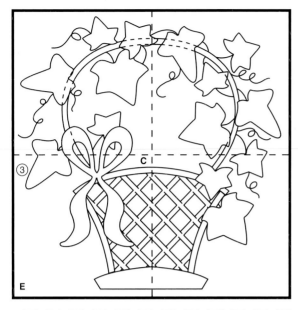

PATTERN #16: "Ivy Basket with Bow"

Third page

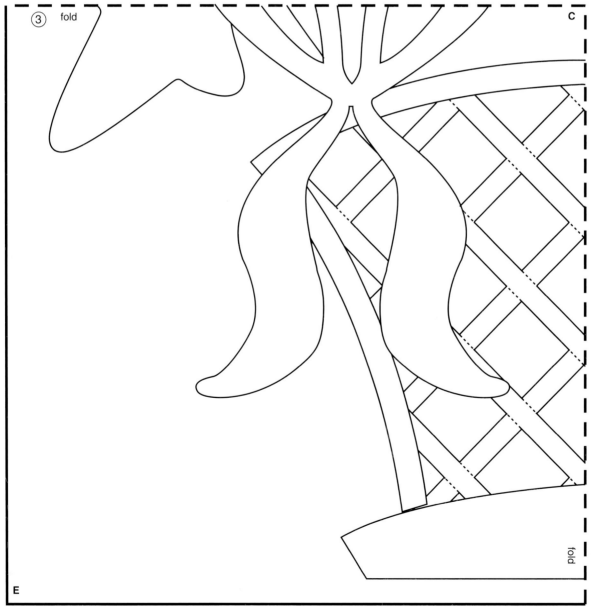

PATTERN #16: "Ivy Basket with Bow"

Fourth page

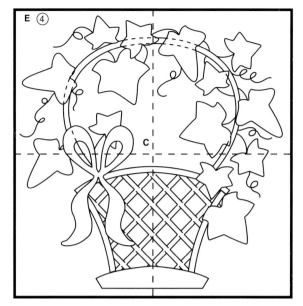

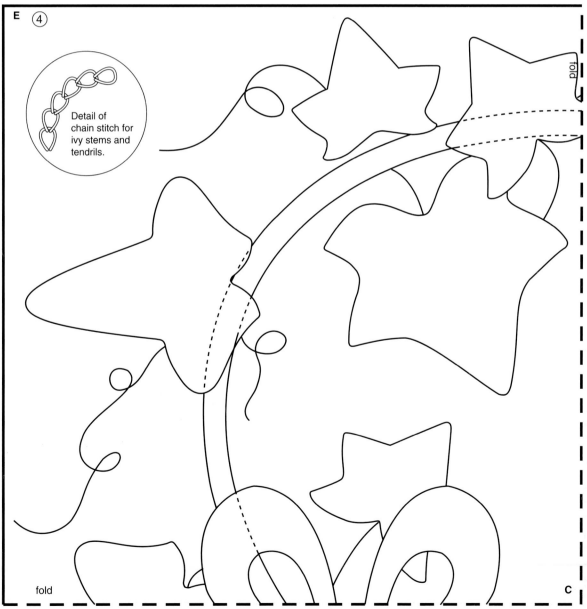

Detail of chain stitch for ivy stems and tendrils.

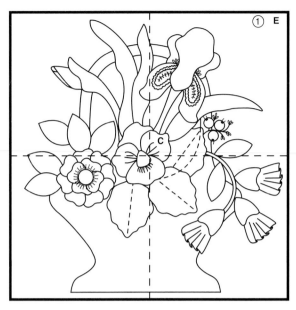

PATTERN #17: "Jeannie's Iris, Pansy, and Pleated Flowers Basket"

Type: "Beyond"; Designed by Jeannie Austin (with Raenell Doyle's basket)

To make this block, refer to Lesson 5; in *Volume I,* Lessons 9 and 10.

The simplest of baskets—a one-piece shape—and a freshly picked spring bouquet, make this block endearing. Jeannie Austin's strong individual style sings when one is privileged to see numbers of her pieces. Some of that song can be caught here. Jeannie's colors—both delicate and vibrant—also have a special style that draw us to them. And she has characteristic details that, shared here in this pattern, will enter our late-20th century Albums. The tiny embroidery accented blueberries recur in her bouquets as do judiciously thread-decorated floral elements.

PATTERN #17: "Jeannie's Iris, Pansy, and Pleated Flowers Basket"

Second page

Jeannie's iris sports a lush beard: double-layered, fringed (raw-edged) bias strips have been gathered down their length and attached to the petal with looped sewing thread. Just by studying the pattern, one can almost picture banks of these sherbet-colored hybrid "flags," which reappear each Spring, full of new life and joyful promise. Jeannie attributes her basket shape to Raenell Doyle, a friend and teacher.

Trace the basket pattern off first, marking half of it on a sheet of paper folded in half lengthwise. Then cut the basket out on the fold. Jeannie's pattern shapes and arrangements are simple enough to be machine sewn. Her basket, leaves, and stems could be mock hand-appliquéd (see Harriet Hargrave's *Mastering Machine Appliqué*). Then one could have the pleasure of doing

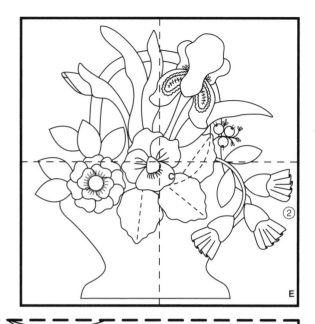

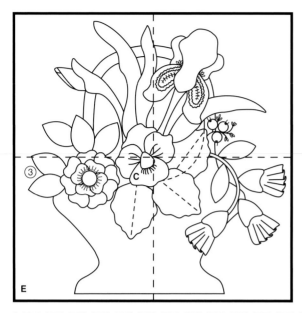

PATTERN #17: "Jeannie's Iris, Pansy, and Pleated Flowers Basket"

Third page

the flowers and embellishments by hand. Consider this time economizer if you choose to pair this Iris basket pattern with Jeannie's "Regal Bird" basket as an elegant set of boudoir or parlor pictures or pillows.

Baltimore Beauties Fabric Notes: For this simple basket shape, the Basketweave prints would work wonderfully. And because they coordinate so appealingly with the three dozen or so prints of the rest of the line, you could pick the Basketweave's colorway first, then build your block (or even your quilt) around that color choice.

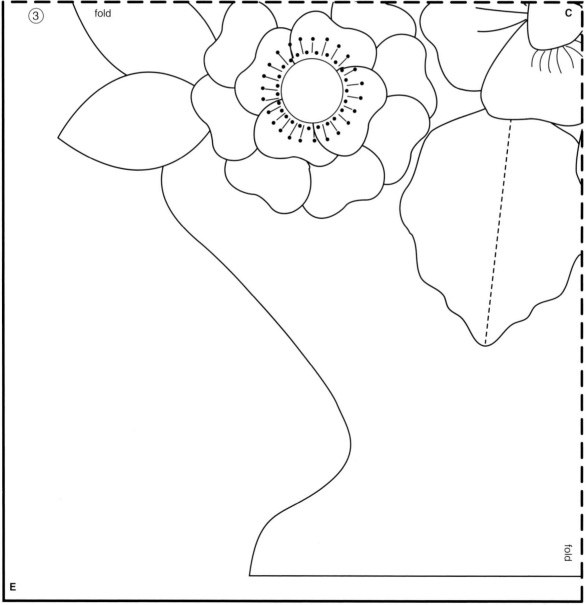

**PATTERN #17: "Jeannie's Iris, Pansy, and
Pleated Flowers Basket"**

Fourth page

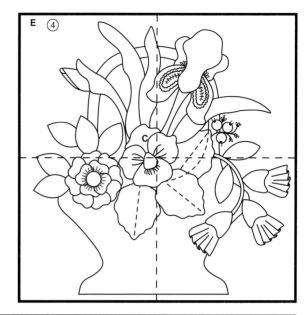

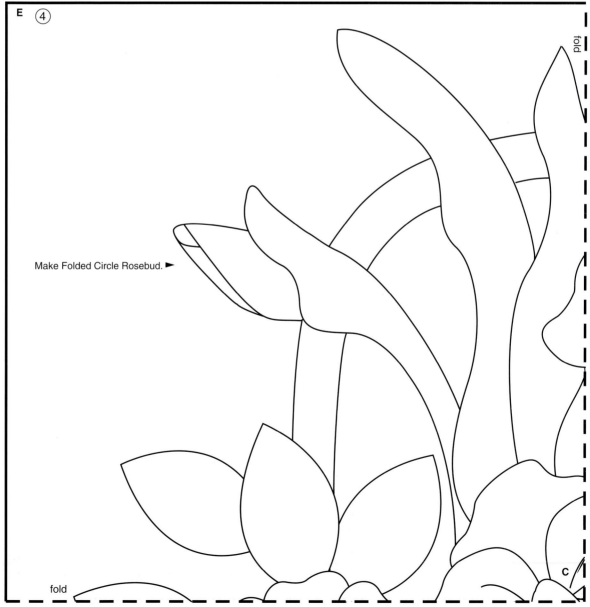

Make Folded Circle Rosebud. ▶

fold

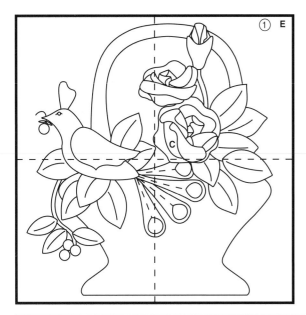

PATTERN #18: "Regal Bird Amidst the Roses"

Type: "Beyond"; Designed by Jeannie Austin (with Raenell Doyle's basket)

To make this block, refer to Lesson 5; in *Volume I*, Lessons 5, 9 and 10.

Using the same Raenell Doyle-inspired basket shape, Jeannie has designed a slightly more formal block than her preceding "Iris, Pansy, and Pleated Flowers" one. While the basket shape and construction remain utterly simple, the arrangement in the basket has a more formal elegance to it. The fulsome dimensional roses, the regally exotic peacock, and the studied, artful placement of bird and blooms within the basket all conspire to make a most appealing *nouvelle* Victorian pattern. And it is a relatively easy one at that! For those of us who enjoy

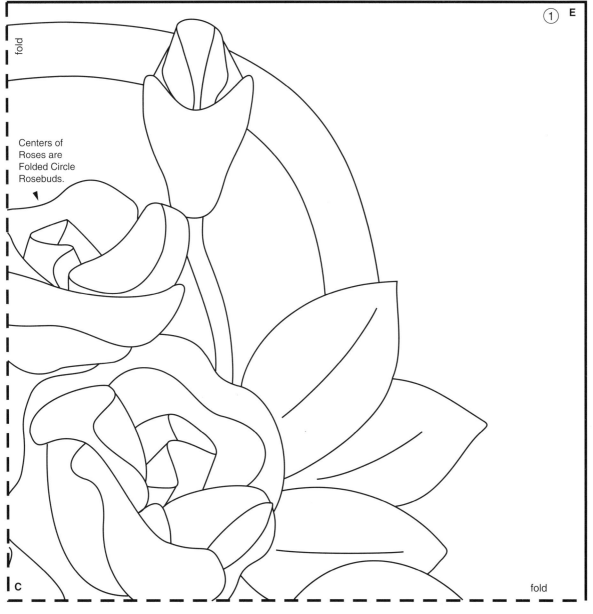

Centers of Roses are Folded Circle Rosebuds.

PATTERN #18: "Regal Bird Amidst the Roses"

Second page

original design, this concept of repeating the basic graphic basket shape, but changing the arrangement in each, might lead to a basket Album based on a similarly consistent theme.

Baltimore Beauties Fabric Notes: Background fabrics sometimes changed in the antique Albums. (One memorable antebellum block has a square of wee rosebuds behind the appliquéd image, then a narrow border of plain off-white fabric frames it.) This variety adds interest to an Album. Why not use a painterly selection of these backgrounds from the Baltimore Beauties line? Try the Antique Rosebud print on cappuchino or on pink. Or the Baltimore Rose in white on off-white, the creamery Vermiculate. Try mixing all with the Classic Album Cloth. Emphatic, simpler appliqué shapes like this block's motifs show dramatically against a print-enriched

PATTERN #18: "Regal Bird Amidst the Roses"

Third page

background—inside your Album, beside it in a frilled or prairie-point edged pillow, or framed, Victoriana-like, on the wall above.

Backing Suggestion: If you use a thin batt (like Fairfield Processing's Poly-Fil® Low-Loft batt), you should avoid risking shadowing from a dark or splashy print quilt backing. Thus, any of the prints listed here would be as ideal for the quilt's backing as for the appliquéd blocks' background.

PATTERN #18: "Regal Bird Amidst the Roses"

Fourth page

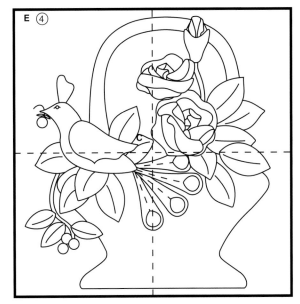

PATTERN #19: "Jeannie's Blue Baltimore Basket"

Type: "Beyond"; Designed by Jeannie Austin

To make this block, refer to Lessons 4 and 5; in *Volume I*, Lessons 9 and 10.

Baskets with an asymmetrically upswept brim were the darlings of old Baltimore. With a sure hand, Jeannie Austin has simplied that basket style down to its basics and colored it blue. With bold, stylized flowers, this basket pattern can be beautifully sewn just as is. Or you can have fun using the basic pattern to hold your own interpretations whether these be in the weaving of the basket or in the fabrication of the blooms. You might, like Sue Linker, sew the blooms of splashy water-colored elements cut from larger prints, or arrange a fulsomely dimensional bouquet of your own picking.

PATTERN #19: "Jeannie's Blue Baltimore Basket"

Second page

PATTERN #19: "Jeannie's Blue Baltimore Basket"

Third page

PATTERN #19: "Jeannie's Blue Baltimore Basket"

Fourth page

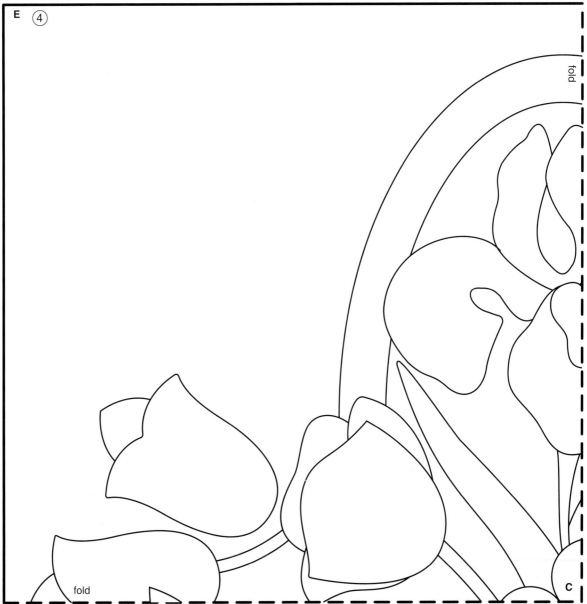

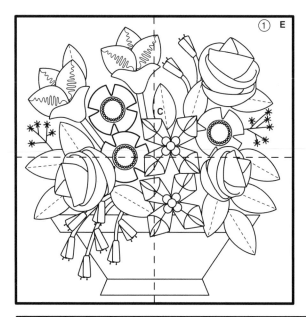

PATTERN #20: "Wilanna's Basket Garden"

Type: "Beyond"; Designed by Wilanna Bristow

To make this block, refer to Lesson 5; in *Volume I*, Lesson 10.

When Charlotte Flesher took up the "basket challenge" (Lesson 6), she invited Wilanna Bristow, a noted San Antonio needleartist, to design a block, too. "Wilanna's Basket Garden" is the generous result. It teaches us some delightfully fresh, very clever techniques. These bountiful offerings appear in this buoyant basket bouquet. Its less familiar flowers are detailed in Lesson 5. The large circles are "Template-free Flowers" from *Volume I*, their centers trimmed round with French knots, which can be made of heavy rope silk or mercerized rope cotton (perle cotton). All of the embroidered embellishment in this block is done in heavy floss. Each leaf, for example, is back-stitched

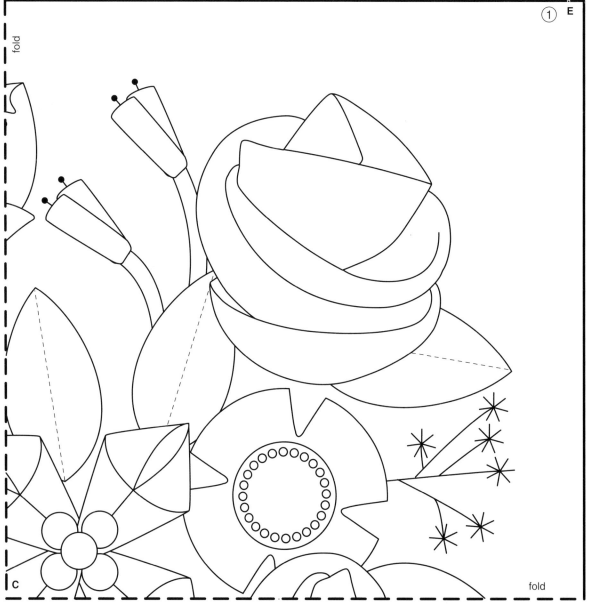

PATTERN #20: "Wilanna's Basket Garden"

Second page

up the center vein. The small "bell" flowers have a ½"-long straight-stitch, which ends in a French knot wrapped once around the thread. The sprays of filler flowers bloom on laid rope cotton (or two strands of perle cotton), couched with fine silk or machine embroidery thread.

The tiny embroidered field flowers can be done in the *mille fleur* stitch. To do this stitch, imagine a circle with a ³⁄₁₆" radius around its center point. With a single strand of perle cotton, stitch from the center to the edge of the circle, repeatedly, eight times. *A variant of this eight-legged stitch:* Sew an X from the top to the bottom of the circle. Then stitch a second X from the left to the right side of the circle. These next two runs across the circle also anchor its center: Each stitch of

Detail of Basket Brim and Base.

PATTERN #20: "Wilanna's Basket Garden"

Third page

the second X takes a back stitch over, under (with a stitch into and out of the background), and over the center of the X again, before it reaches the other side of the circle and re-enters the cloth.

Studying how this block was made was a thrill. Wilanna's techniques differ dramatically from those in traditional quiltmaking. Their effectiveness belies the ease with which they are made. Wilanna knows a vast amount about threads and cloth—grain, texture, weight, and weave—and when to cut on the bias or the straight. Where the technique allows it, she is quick and economical with her stitches. Wilanna clearly has a wealth of innovative possibilities to infuse into traditional quiltmaking.

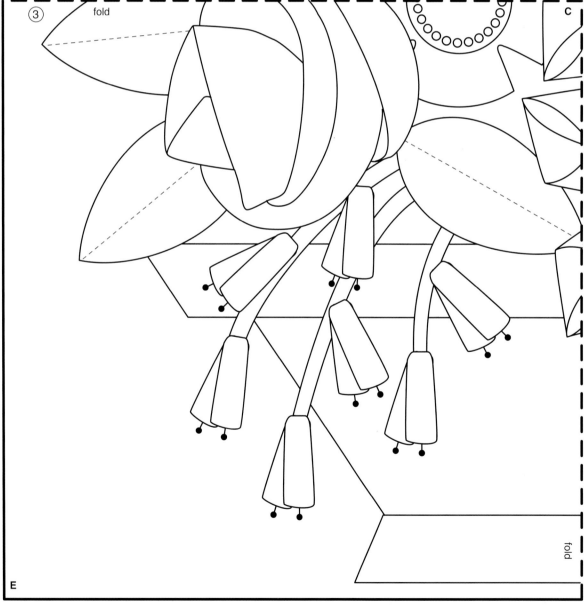

PATTERN #20: "Wilanna's Basket Garden"

Fourth page

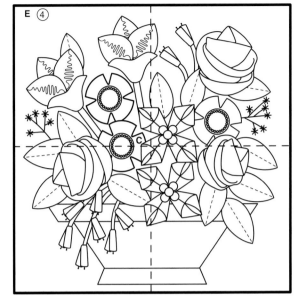

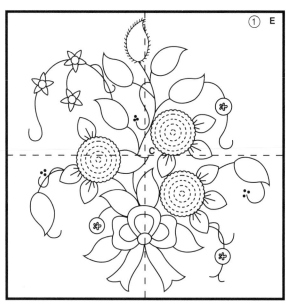

PATTERN #21: "Baltimore Bouquet"

Type: "Beyond"; Designed by Gwendolyn LeLacheur

To make this block, refer to Lessons 3, 7, and 8; in *Volume I*, Lessons 5, 8, and 10.

Gwen suggests this approach to her block:

1. Appliqué the bow and all the leaves except the gathered leaves, which lie under the ruched roses. (Gwen's instructions for her gathered leaves are shared in Lesson 8.)

2. Ruched Roses *(Volume I, Lesson 8)*.

Key:

1. Stem Stitch   2. Petals-on-a-String   3. Gathered Leaves
4. Yo-Yo Posey   5. Ruched Rose   6. Blanket-Stitched Leaves
7. French Knots   8. Triple Bowknot Ribbon

PATTERN #21: "Baltimore Bouquet"

Second page

3. Yo-Yos: Trace around a large spool of thread onto fabric. Cut out with a ¼" seam allowance. Turn the raw edge to the wrong side on the drawn line. Stitch this hem with small running stitches. Pull thread to gather and backstitch to hold the gathers. Stitch through the yo-yo's center with matching thread to sew it to the background. Tuck in a fringed center (Lesson 2).

4. Petals-on-a-String (instructions in Lesson 8).

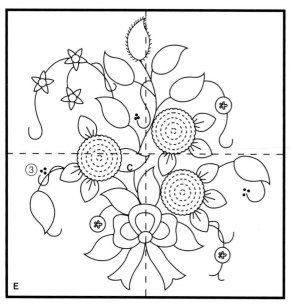

PATTERN #21: "Baltimore Bouquet"

Third page

PATTERN #21: "Baltimore Bouquet"

Fourth page

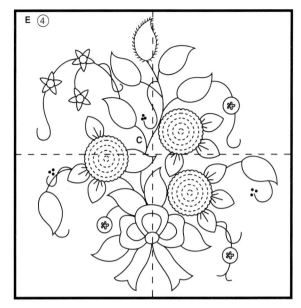

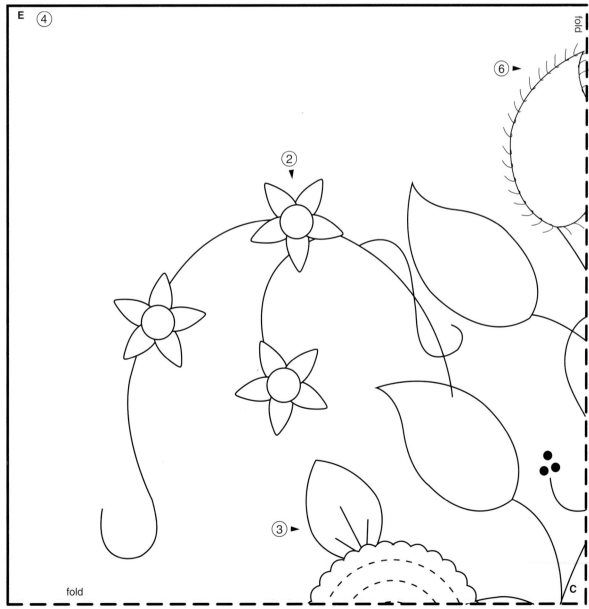

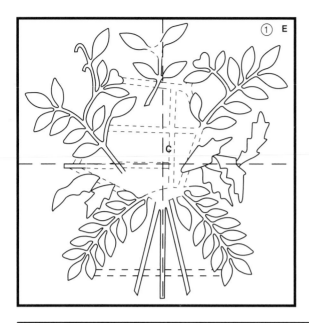

PATTERN #22 "Numsen Bouquet I: Foliage Pattern"

Type: "Beyond"; Designed by the author

To make this block, refer to Lessons 9 and 10; in *Volume I*, Lessons 2, 5, 8, and 10.

This is the cut-away appliqué pattern for the greenery used in both Nancy Hornback's interpretation of the Numsen Bouquet and mine. Except for the horizontal row of jagged Christmas Cactus leaves in the center of the block, all the other leaves and stems were sewn by the "cut-away appliqué" technique: a freezer paper pattern is affixed to the right side of the fabric, and you cut out the appliqué a few inches at a time as you sew it in place. Just beyond the edge of the freezer paper is the seam fold line. Using a large-scale print for most of the leaves and stems belies the fact that they are sewn from one piece. The print itself makes the block look much more complicated than it is. Stitch the greenery first, then choose flowers to ornament your version of this

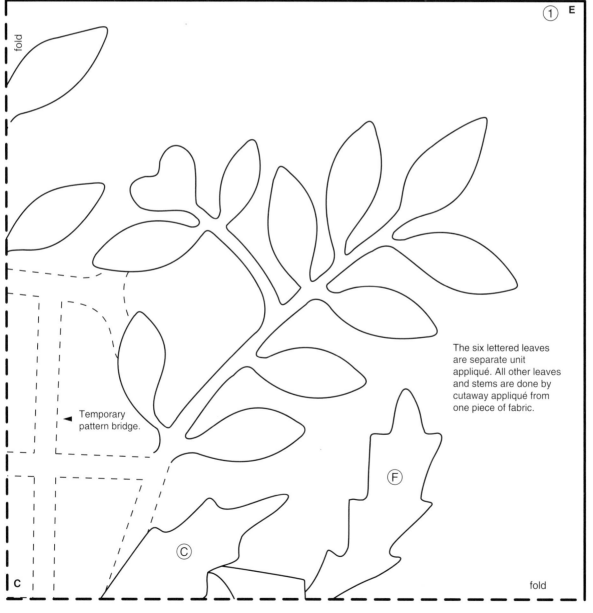

The six lettered leaves are separate unit appliqué. All other leaves and stems are done by cutaway appliqué from one piece of fabric.

◄ Temporary pattern bridge.

PATTERN #22 "Numsen Bouquet I: Foliage Pattern"

Second page

block. A placement diagram for both "Numsen Family Bouquet Revisited" and "Beribboned Bouquet" are given here with legends showing which flowers occur where. With the greenery stitched, you will place the flowers by eye.

Review the lessons in *Volume I* on using freezer paper on the top, and "pattern bridges."

Baltimore Beauties Fabric Note: The P & B fabric, whose design the author worked on for this series, has several pieces ideal for the Numsen Bouquet's foliage. If you'd like the restful monochromatic green of Nancy Hornback's block, choose one of the Vermiculate greens. If you prefer a big, broken-up print, like the author's "Beribboned Bouquet" foliage, try the green colorway of the Ombré Leaves or the Baltimore Rose prints.

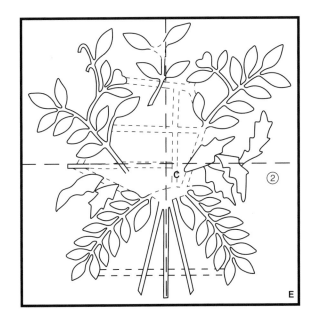

PATTERN #22 "Numsen Bouquet I: Foliage Pattern"

Third page

Key to #22, Numsen Family Bouquet Revisited (interpretation made by Nancy Hornback):

1. Ruched Flowers   2. Folded Circle Rosebuds
3. Mrs. Numsen's Rose II   4. Tucked-Circle Rosebuds
5. Bluebells

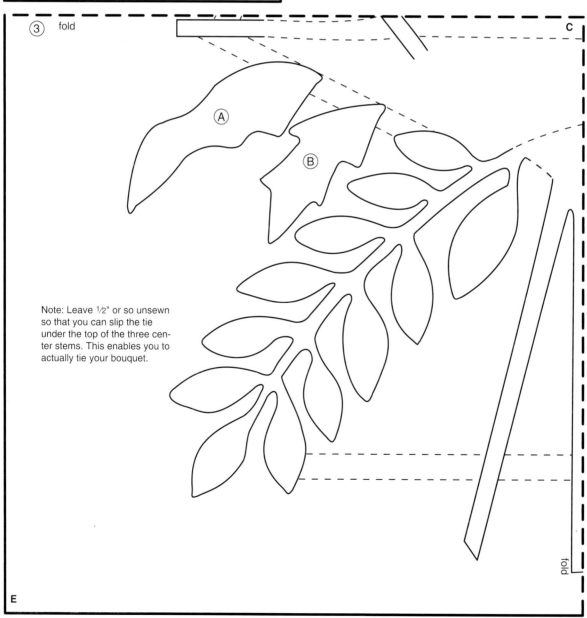

Note: Leave 1/2" or so unsewn so that you can slip the tie under the top of the three center stems. This enables you to actually tie your bouquet.

PATTERN #22 "Numsen Bouquet I: Foliage Pattern"

Fourth page

Key to #22, Numsen Bouquet III: Beribboned Bouquet (interpretation made by the author):

1. Ruched Ribbon Camelia
2. Rolled-Wire Ribbon Rose (Method #2)
3. Rolled-Wire Ribbon Rose (Method #3)   4. Primroses
5. Mrs. Numsen's Rose III   6. Tucked-Circle Rosebuds
7. Bluebells   8. Peony Bud   9. Lily of the Valley
10. Christmas Cactus Bud

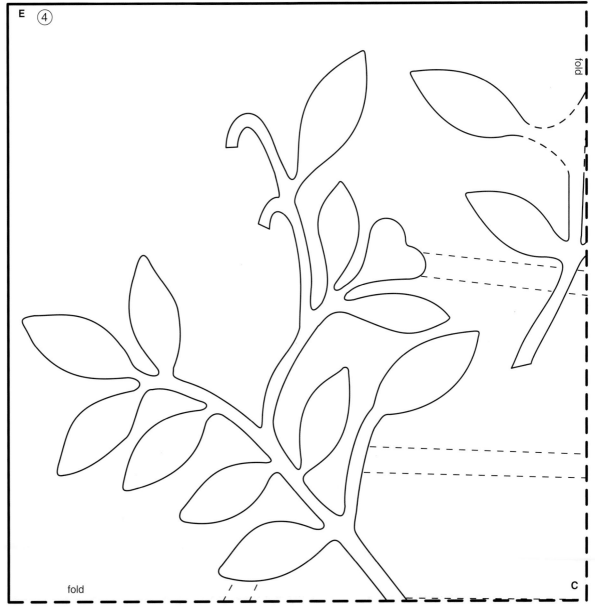

PATTERN #23: "Texas Treasures"

Type: "Beyond"; Designed by J. Jane Mc. Mitchell

To make this block, refer to Lessons 4 and 6; in *Volume I*, Lessons 5, 9, and 10. Also see Appendix I in *Baltimore Album Quilts—Historic Notes and Antique Patterns.*

An Iris, Texas Bluebonnets, and the Yellow Rose of Texas all bloom from Jane's beautiful original design block. Taking inspiration from a traditional Baltimore pattern, Jane has made one of those blocks that seems simply perfect. The basket is a restrained weaving of three wine reds: a solid, a pindot, and a geometric. The flowers show close observation of nature. Their gestures are realistically appliquéd, and their characteristic details finely embroidered in sewing thread. Color and shape, cloth and texture are skillfully melded into a block so lovely that it adorns this book's cover.

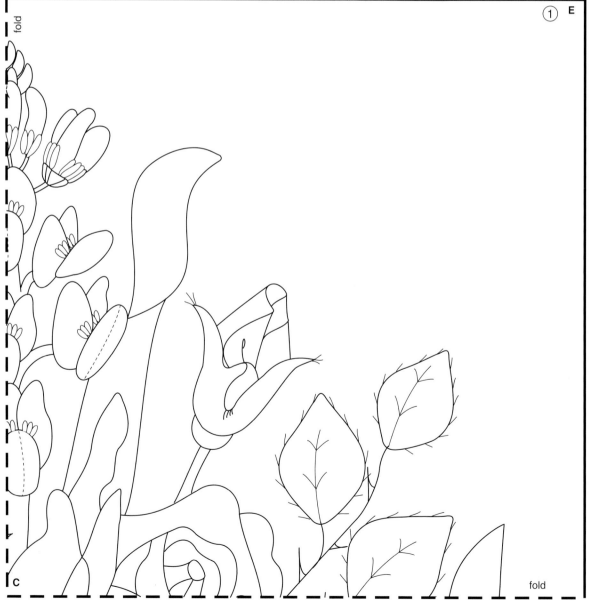

PATTERN #23: "Texas Treasures"

Second page

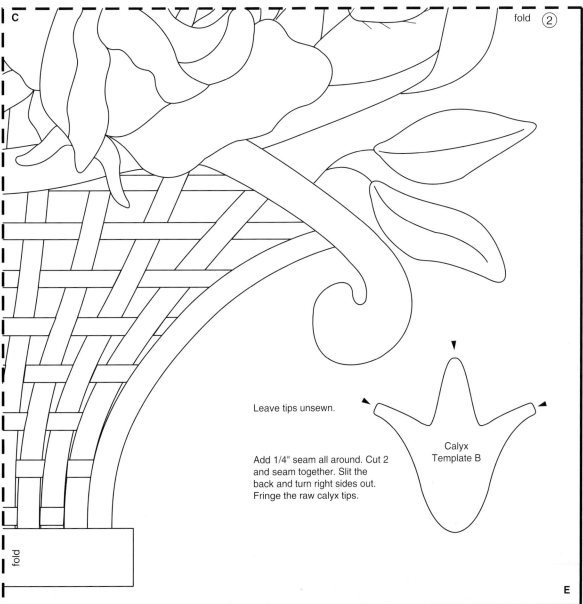

Leave tips unsewn.

Add 1/4" seam all around. Cut 2 and seam together. Slit the back and turn right sides out. Fringe the raw calyx tips.

Calyx
Template B

fold

C

fold ②

E

PATTERN #23: "Texas Treasures"

Third page

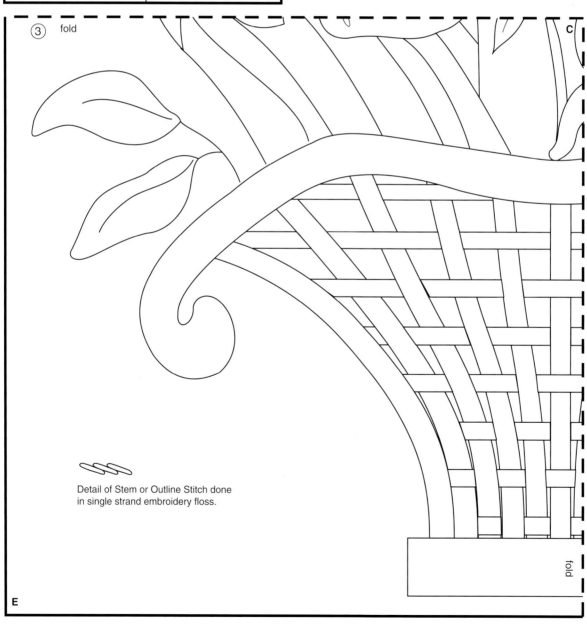

Detail of Stem or Outline Stitch done
in single strand embroidery floss.

PATTERN #23: "Texas Treasures"

Fourth page

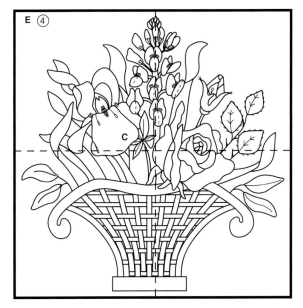

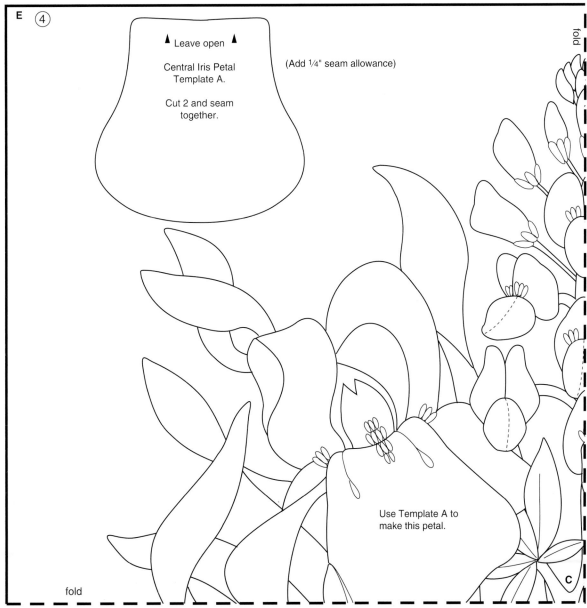

E ④

▲ Leave open ▲

Central Iris Petal
Template A.

Cut 2 and seam
together.

(Add ¼" seam allowance)

Use Template A to
make this petal.

fold

fold

C

PATTERN #24A: "Fancy Flowers"

Type: "Beyond"; Designed by the author

To make this block, refer to Lessons 3, 8, 9; in *Volume I*, Lessons 6, 7, 8, 9, 10, and 11.

This ornate block was taught in a series article in *Quilter's Newsletter Magazine* and is the subject of Lesson 9. All of the techniques are covered either in this book's lessons, or in *Volume I*. The Key points to the techniques used, while the lessons where these methods appear are cited above. A second vase (pattern #24B) is shown with half of its pattern to cut on the fold (on page 159). This second vase is the one from that antique original, which inspired me to design and make this block. Use whichever vase you choose, and fill it full with the fancy flowers your heart desires.

PATTERN #24A: "Fancy Flowers"

Second page

Key to this block's techniques:

1. Superfine Stem Variation   2. *Broderie Perse* Leaf   3. Stuffed Silk Roses
4. Template-Free Flowers   5. Inked Embellishments
6. Thread Embellishments   7. Top-Stitching   8. Blanket-Stitching
9. Perfect Grapes   10. Ruched Flowers (Yellow Zinnias for "thoughts of absent friends")
11. Reverse Appliqué for tulip petals and cut-glass details on the Vase
12. Rick Rack Roses   13. Folded-Circle Rosebuds

PATTERN #24A: "Fancy Flowers"

Third page

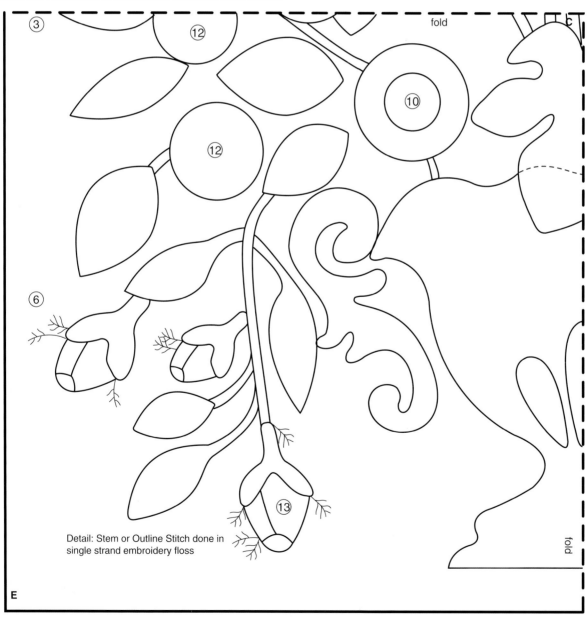

Detail: Stem or Outline Stitch done in
single strand embroidery floss

PATTERN #24A: "Fancy Flowers"

Fourth page

PATTERN #24B
Optional Vase

Place Pattern
on fold.

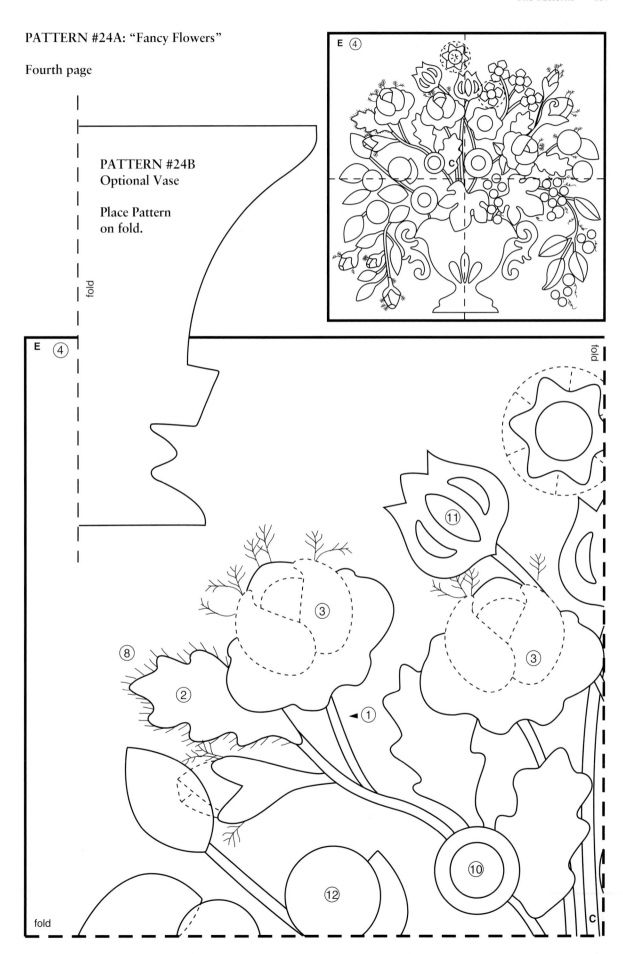

PATTERN #26: "Rita Kilstrom's Round Basket"

Type: "Beyond"; Designed by Rita Kilstrom

Quite bold and modern-looking, this basket has the mass needed to hold heavy ribbon flower blooms beautifully.

PATTERN #26

PATTERN #25: "Victorian Weave Basket"

Type: "Beyond"; By Carol Spalding

Patterns #25 through #33 are all contemporary basket patterns. To make these baskets, refer to Lessons 2 through 6; in *Volume I*, Lesson 9.

Carol has combined warps of pre-turned cotton bias stems with weavers of narrow silk "ribbon-floss" in an exquisite basket.

PATTERN #25

PATTERN #27: "Pedestal Basket with Handle"

Type: "Beyond"; Designed by the author

Three stems twist to form the brim's valley, then extend to braided handles on this basket. The braided vertical handle is optional and would best be sewn down after the basket is filled so that it passes over, then appears to go behind, the contents.

Continue the braid in an arc to form the handle.

PATTERN #27

PATTERN #28: "Annie Tuley's Pleated Basket"

Type: "Beyond"; Designed by Annie Tuley

This effective basket was made with Clotilde's Perfect Pleater®.

PATTERN #28

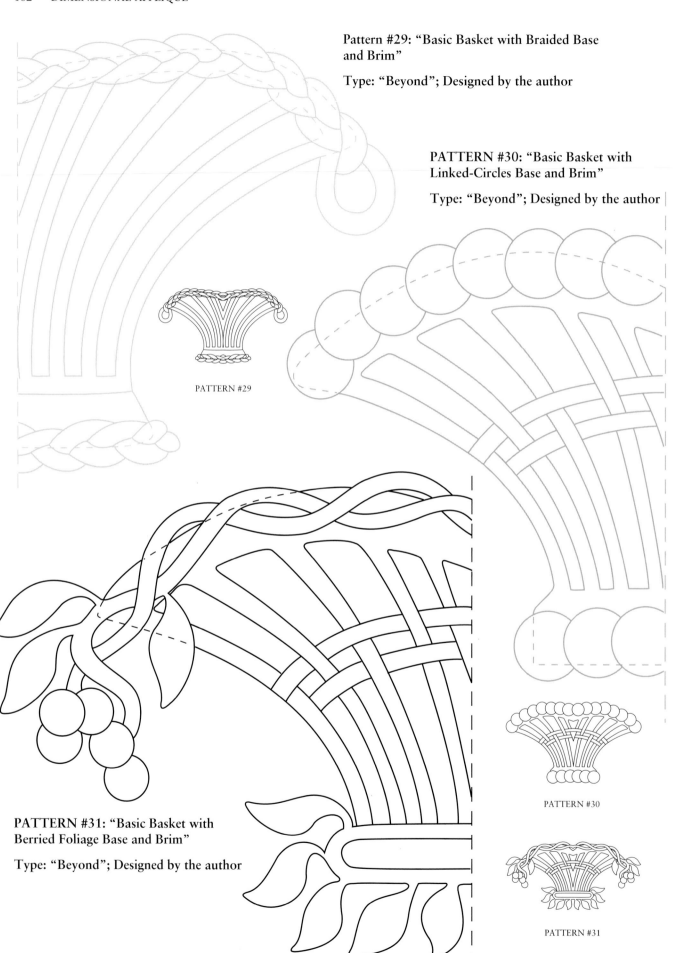

Pattern #29: "Basic Basket with Braided Base and Brim"

Type: "Beyond"; Designed by the author

PATTERN #30: "Basic Basket with Linked-Circles Base and Brim"

Type: "Beyond"; Designed by the author

PATTERN #29

PATTERN #31: "Basic Basket with Berried Foliage Base and Brim"

Type: "Beyond"; Designed by the author

PATTERN #30

PATTERN #31

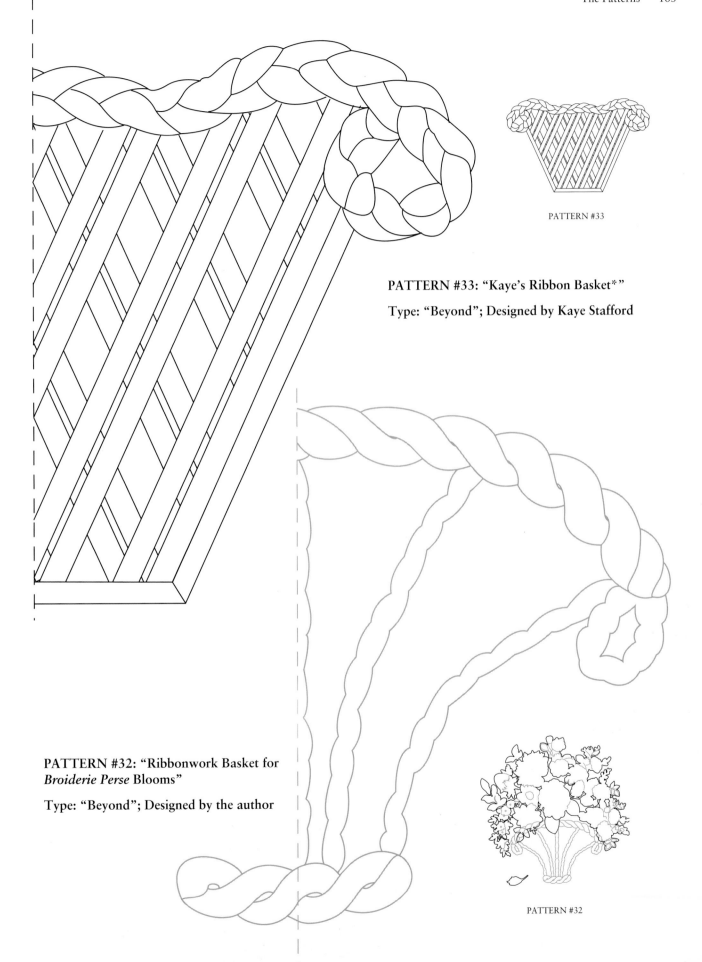

PATTERN #33

PATTERN #33: "Kaye's Ribbon Basket*"

Type: "Beyond"; Designed by Kaye Stafford

PATTERN #32: "Ribbonwork Basket for *Broiderie Perse* Blooms"

Type: "Beyond"; Designed by the author

PATTERN #32

STITCHERY GARDEN, abloom with dimension and designed by
Charlotte Flesher. No pattern given. (Photo: S. Risedorph)

Part Four: The Quiltmakers

About the Contemporary Needleartists whose work appears in *Dimensional Appliqué — Baskets, Blooms, and Baltimore Borders*. When a quiltmaker has offered to contribute stitchery time, talent, or a photo of her piece to the *Baltimore Beauties* series, she fills out a short questionnaire for the series' archival notebooks. The following short biographies are taken from material thus provided. *Note:* Biographical notes on needleartists generally appear only once in the series even though their work may appear in several volumes.

A TOKEN OF GRATITUDE, by Cleda Dawson. (Pattern #17 from *Volume I*). (Photo: S. Risedorph)

JEANNIE AUSTIN of Graham, Washington: Regal Bird Amidst the Roses; Jeannie's Blue Baltimore Basket; and Jeannie's Iris, Pansy, and Pleated Flowers Basket.

"Appliqué is my 'passion.' My favorite way to work is straight from my head onto the fabric, using strong colors and simple shapes. I enjoy studying the history of quilting and quilters—especially the 'Baltimore' era, with its lavish Victorian overabundance. This is totally opposite to the way I live and work—and I LOVE it!"

DEBRA L. BALLARD of Midland, Michigan: Crown of Ten Penny Roses.

"Quiltmaking has been passed down to me through my paternal grandmother.... Quilts were on all our beds because of these women.... Now I find myself teaching and presenting lectures. I presented a paper to the American Quilt Study Group in 1989—a highlight in my quilting pursuits. I find the history of quilting is fascinating."

MELODY BOLLAY of Santa Barbara, California: Basket of Quarter Roses and Buds.

Melody has lived in Santa Barbara most of her life. She studied biology in college and taught marine biology (her special interest) and oceanography at a local school. "I 'went through' embroidery, knitting, weaving, and rug-hooking," Melody writes, "before settling down to quilting, especially appliqué."

WILANNA BRISTOW of San Antonio, Texas: Wilanna's Basket Garden.

A stitcher since childhood, Wilanna's focus is on art, color, embroidery, and appliqué. With a BFA degree, she teaches and is a Certified Judge for the Embroiderers' Guild of America. Her work is in the Library of the Costume Institute of the Metropolitan Museum, New York City, and in the Archives of American Art, Washington, D.C. Wilanna's classes cover dimensional flowers and stitchery.

JENIFER BUECHEL of Pittsburgh, Pennsylvania: A Token of Remembrance.

"I love the challenge of designing original pieces and am encouraged in this by a special friend and wonderful family. My work combines my two favorite loves: calligraphy and appliqué with varied techniques. I have won a few awards for my work (including a viewers' choice) and teach here at the Quilt Shoppe."

MARSHA CARTER of Orange, California: Unadorned Victorian Basket of Flowers.

"I began quiltmaking in 1987 out of a need for a hobby, taking classes through adult education. Winning second prize in my first block contest convinced me that I wanted to be a professional quiltmaker. I now teach classes on a full-time basis, deriving great satisfaction from passing on my love and skill in the art of making quilts."

GLADYS CLAYSON of Camino, California: Crown of Chintz Roses.

"I have been around quilting all my life. I remember playing under the quilt frame during quilting bees when I was a little girl. I began making quilts in high school for older friends getting married and later having babies. Appliqué is my favorite kind of quilting now. I often design my own patterns, and I have taught quilting classes."

CLEDA J. DAWSON of Jefferson, Oregon: Token of Gratitude.

"I started my first quilt at age 8. I now do professional hand quilting. I've raised three children, buried one, and have a 10-year-old at home. I am basically a self-taught quilter except for hand-appliqué. I love color and use an intuitive approach. The process of working with color takes on a life of its own and creates an unstoppable momentum."

CHARLOTTE FLESHER of San Antonio, Texas: Stitchery Garden.

"It's hard to say which I enjoy most, the making of the quilts or the teaching and sharing with others. I have taught quiltmaking since 1968. The 3-D 'Fancy' flowers so popular now are very much like the calico flowers my sister Vicki Dishon and I made and sold in craft booths in the '60s while we tried to get people interested in our quilts, classes, and patterns." On April 1, 1993, Charlotte died at age 50.

WENDY GRANDE of Aptos, California: Folk Art Basket of Flowers.

Wendy's quilting provides expression in color, form, and texture. She is inspired by all around her—her family, their vacations, and the work of other quilters. It is important to Wendy to preserve needlework, knitting, crochet, tatting, ribbon work, and fine hand sewing. But she always comes home to quilting.

ROSLYN HAY (formerly Kempston) of Richardson, Texas: Flowers From Home.

"My sewing ability comes naturally, as both grandparents were tailors. My school teacher, Mrs. James, won me forever to sewing by age 8." Roslyn has been in the United States 14 years and has been a stellar influence in the Dallas Quilters' Guild and Sharon's Quilting Depot where she teaches. When she returns, soon, to Sydney, Australia, she'll plant new seeds, and more appliqué flowers will bloom!

MARJO HODGES of Danville, California: Crown of Quilted Roses.

"I began sewing at the young age of 5 with my brother. I never stopped, but changed directions to quiltmaking. My desire to learn more has taken me to workshops and lectures across the country. My true challenge is in the beauty of the finished Baltimore Album blocks." (See more of Marjo's work in *Volume III*.)

NANCY HORNBACK of Wichita, Kansas: Numsen Family Bouquet Revisited.

"I began making quilts in 1973 and taught myself from library books. I am a past President of the Prairie Quilt Guild of Wichita and co-founder of the Kansas Quilt Project: Documenting Quilts and Quiltmakers. I am particularly interested in appliqué quilts of the 19th century."

IRENE KEATING of Alameda, California: Ivy Basket with Bow.

"The block is my own design. The ivy patterns came from the good Lord himself as I would gather ivy leaves while walking the dog. I simply put them on the photocopying machine and presto! patterns!" Irene is a prolific stitcher, sewing her time into beauty as she accompanies her husband on his business travels.

RITA YOUNG KILSTROM of Arnold, California: Rita Kilstrom's Round Basket.

"My sewing interest was sparked by my eighth-grade home economics class. In addition to baby, wall, and bed quilts, I've made one for the AIDS Names Quilt Project. Currently I'm leading our guild through my pieced basket block with appliquéd Sierra wildflowers (our 1993 'donation quilt'). I belong to the Network for Wearable Art, and sell custom-designed clothing."

BONNIE CLIFTON KNEZO of Roswell, Georgia: Flower-Wreathed Heart.

Bonnie's initiation into needlework began during law school as a means to alleviate stress. Later, involvement in the EGA introduced her to the delicate art of French handsewing and fine embroidery. Her first experience in quiltmaking and appliqué came through a year-long study of Baltimore Album quilts.

MARJORIE KRUTY of Hempstead, New York: Wreath of Stuffed Roses.

As a former English teacher and mother of five,

Marjorie's "fascination for needlework was kindled when my aunt began bringing home flannel scraps from the factory where she worked. As a child I remember pinning the scraps in various positions on a celluloid doll.... I am especially fond of hand appliqué and embroidery [because they] always reinstate my basic values of perseverance and patience."

GWENDOLYN S. LELACHEUR of Harsen's Island, Michigan: Roses are Red, I Promised You a Rose Garden, Rick Rack Roses, and Baltimore Bouquet.

A quiltmaking teacher, designer and NQA certified judge, Gwen writes, "Quilting professionally affords me the opportunity to be at work and play at the same time! There are always new color schemes, designs, and techniques to explore. I am pleased to see so many quilters returning to fine hand-appliqué, due to the Baltimore Album quilt revival."

SUE LINKER of Sumner, Washington: Basket of Flowers Wall Hanging, Ferns and Floribunda Roses, and Jeannie's Blue Baltimore Basket.

"My quiltmaking preference is handwork, and my passion is appliqué. My primary focus is teaching. Quilters are wonderful, caring, sharing people. It pleases me most to have people accomplish what they thought they couldn't do, expand their visions, and not be afraid to break some rules." (Judged by the wealth of Sue's contributions to this book, her classes are wonderful!)

J. JANE MC. MITCHELL of Dallas, Texas: Texas Treasures.

"I learned to quilt in 1983 as a result of my childhood love for quilts. I have won awards for my quilts, but I am proudest of the blue ribbon I won at the Dallas Quilt Show for an heirloom quilted wedding dress I made for my eldest daughter. I am co-owner of Sharon's Quilt Depot in the historic city of McKinney located north of Dallas, Texas.... This [our cover block] is my first original appliqué block...."

BARBARA L. PUDIAK of Fairport, New York: Spring Basket Wall Quilt.

"I began sewing when I was 8. My mom, the daughter of immigrant Italians, worked in a sweatshop in her youth and sewed very well. ...I started quilting in 1985, opened my shop, Pins and Needles, in 1989. It's now in my home and is a real family business run by my husband Steve (who helps design our appliqués) and our 4-year-old son, Dylan."

HEIDI CHESLEY SANDBERG of Cape Elizabeth, Maine: Vase of Full Blown Roses.

"I began sewing when I was 5 and have been enjoying all types of needlework ever since. After graduating with a degree in textiles and two years of teaching, I represent fabric and notion companies. My profession is a joy to me as my work and my interests have merged as one." (Heidi represents P & B's "Baltimore Beauties" designer fabric, which debuts with this book.)

BEVERLY FRIEDLINE SCHIAVONI of Pacific Grove, California: Beverly's Beauty.

"At a very young age, my mom taught me how to make doll clothes and from there I have sewed all my life. After a nursing career and raising four children, I began to make traditional quilts. I've...[won] many ribbons and prizes for my quilts and am still making doll clothes for my collection of early rag and art fabric dolls."

CAROL SPALDING of Oakhurst, California: Blessings of Autumn (Victorian Weave Basket)

After years of drawing and painting, Carol turned to the medium of fiber art. She applied her artistic ability first to piecing fabric and then turned to traditional appliqué and *broderie perse*, where she found more freedom of expression. She imitates with fabric the various forms and shapes of nature. An award-winning artist, Carol lives and works in Oakhurst, California.

KAYE STAFFORD of Riverton, Wyoming: Kaye's Ribbon Basket.

Kaye has as sure a sense of design as she does of purpose. She designed this striking basket in a class at Asilomar in California. Arriving with a unique selection of materials, she proceeded to turn the forest green cloth and ribbon into a basket so striking that we share its pattern here.

ELIZABETH ANNE TAYLOR of Dallas, Texas: Home Grown Bouquet.

"I was born in outback New South Wales and have been stitching for as long as I can remember.

My mother taught me at first and later, after moving to Sydney, I learned quilting and all kinds of embroidery. When I came to Dallas, I discovered appliqué. I'll be returning home with wonderful memories of America and an addiction to appliqué quilts."

YOLANDA TOVAR of Boca Raton, Florida: Flower-Wreathed Heart with Pansies.

Born in Boston and raised in Caracas, Venezuela, Yolanda was taught needle skills as a child by French nuns. She excels in embroidery, precision hand appliqué, intricate piecing, *broderie perse*, smocking, and quilting. Inspiration for her work comes from many sources, including the study of historic costumes, architecture, and drawings. Yolanda is an exceptional artist, honored by a blue ribbon and prizes. She is expanding her horizons dramatically today as she pursues a professional art/psychology career. She collaborated with Barbara Hahl on a magnificent gift for this series, an Album medallion couched in gold thread. Its pattern appears in *Appliqué 12 Borders and Medallions* (1994).

ANNIE TULEY of Export, Pennsylvania: Blue Album, and Annie Tuley's Pleated Basket.

"My mother and grandmother, at my insistence, taught me to sew when I was 5 years old. ...I have enjoyed the challenges of adapting the beautiful traditional techniques to the time-saving modern sewing machines. I hope that in passing on new techniques, just as our grandmothers did, women of the future will continue making quilts, rather than giving up because 'there just isn't enough time.' "

YVONNE VON NIEDA of Temple Hills, Maryland: Ribbonwork Basket for *Broderie Perse* Blooms

Yvonne's needlework started when her grandmother taught her to knit at about age 7. In high school she took sewing and fell in love with the buttonhole stitch. Since her first quilting class six years ago, she is determined to make a large quilt for each of her grandchildren to have when he or she grows up.

Appendix I: Course Descriptions & Album Quilt Teachers

The following descriptions of ten possible quilting classes use *Dimensional Appliqué—Baskets, Blooms, and Baltimore Borders* as a textbook and pattern source. Anyone who would like to teach these course formats or who would like to use these course descriptions and materials lists verbatim has the author's and the publisher's permission to do so. Since this book's copyright notices prohibit photocopying or other printing of any other material herein, *Dimensional Appliqué* should always be included in the supply lists for patterns and how-to illustrations. I am always so pleased to hear of any teacher teaching from my books, or of any group of friends working through them as a stitch and study group.

I. A HALF-DAY OR EVENING (THREE-HOUR) COURSE

Fancy Flowers Boutique—Gift making time! Whip up some of the quick-and-easy charmers from Lesson 1 in *Dimensional Appliqué* while making the acquaintance of this delightful gold mine of three-dimensional blooms. **Materials:** Bring *Dimensional Appliqué*, four yards of 1½"-wide wire ribbon, Gem Tac glue, milliner's needle & clear nylon thread. Bring three types of jewelry findings. Bring a 6" square of fabric fused to itself (or man-made leather or felt) to back the flowers, plus a couple of scraps of green fabric for leaves and yellow for centers.

Wreath of Folded Ribbon Roses—An elegant, easy Album Block introduction to using shaded French wire ribbons. Learn the basics of both cut-away appliqué (with or without freezer paper on the top) and ribbon work on this striking wreath. This pattern works as wonderfully for a cushion or inscribed framed hanging as it does for a quilt block. **Materials:** Bring *Dimensional Appliqué*, basic sewing kit (including paper and small cut-to-the point fabric scissors, milliner's #10 or #11 needles, silk pins, ruler, thread to match appliqués, iron, 13" freezer paper), 4½" of 1½"-wide ribbon per rose (the shaded French wire ribbon is ideal), two 16" squares of fabric: one of a leaf/stem green; one of a background of Album cloth. At home, trace Pattern #3 from *Dimensional Appliqué* (centered) onto the front side of the green fabric square.

II. A TWO HALF-DAY OR TWO EVENING (TWO TO THREE HOURS) COURSE

A Wonderfully Quick and Easy Victorian Ribbonwork Album Block—We can almost guarantee you'll finish this beautiful block by the end of class! It is "Victorian Ribbon Basket With Wire Ribbon Roses," Lesson 2 in *Dimensional Appliqué*. We'll make the basket and leaves in the first class, do the roses and inkwork in the second. (This block makes a fabulous decorator item as well, if you'd prefer it as a loveseat cushion or framed under glass on a wall.) **Materials:** Bring *Dimensional Appliqué*, basic sewing kit (including paper and small cut-to-the point fabric scissors, milliner's #10 or #11 needles, silk pins, ruler, thread to match appliqués, ¼" basting tape, gluestick, 13" freezer paper, iron), 1 yard of 1½"-wide ribbon each for four roses (the shaded French wire ribbon is ideal). Bring a 16" background square of Album cloth. At home, trace Pattern #13 from *Dimensional Appliqué* (centered) onto its front side.

III. AN ALL-DAY (FIVE TO SIX HOURS) COURSE

Fancy Ribbon Basketry, *Broderie Perse* **Blooms**—Pamper yourself! Finish an heirloom basket, fuse down the blooms, begin the blanket-stitch edging, then leave class with a fancywork kit all ready to sew for a beautiful Album Block (Lesson 3's block in *Dimensional Appliqué*). **Materials:** Bring *Dimensional Appliqué*, Basic sewing kit, ½ yard of a large floral print (backed with a fusible bonding) suitable for Lesson 3's block, 16" square of Album cloth background, plus the supplies for the block, which are listed at the start of Lesson 3 in *Dimensional Appliqué*.

IV. A THREE HALF-DAY OR THREE EVENING COURSE (THREE THREE-HOUR CLASSES)

Three Basic (But Beautiful!) Baskets—Three is the magic number! We'll meet every third week to get a good start and a fine finish to the three charming basket blocks in Lesson 4 of Elly Sienkiewicz's *Dimensional Appliqué*. Learn Raw-Edged Bias, Overlay Appliqué (both flat and stuffed), Turned-Bias Stems, Latticework Basketry, Speed-Stitching From the Back, Quarter Roses, Tucked-Circle Rosebuds, Chain Stitch and Single-Thread Embroidery. **Materials:** Bring *Dimensional Appliqué*. See Lesson 4 for the materials for "Apples in the Late Afternoon" (Pattern #15) Mark the pattern on the front side of a 16" square of Album cloth and bring to the first class. Also bring the leaves and apples cut out of freezer paper and the cut bias strips for the basket. Materials listed in *Dimensional Appliqué* and the patterns for "Basket of Quarter Roses and Buds" (Pattern #11), and "Ivy Basket with Bow" (Pattern #16) should be brought to the second and third classes

V. A THREE HALF-DAY OR THREE EVENING COURSE (THREE THREE-HOUR CLASSES)

Dimensional Wreaths—Begin a Crown of Roses (a crossed-stem wreath) in each class. Begin your block and clear your path to finishing one of these gorgeous blocks after each session. We'll make the blocks and learn these techniques from Lesson 7 in *Dimensional Appliqué*: Bias Stems, Split Leaves, Ten Penny Roses, Straight-Stitched Leaves, Stuffed Silk Roses, Embroidered Quilting, Two-Color Ruching, Ruching a Rose in your Hand, Five Different Centers for Ruching, and Rolled Ruching. **Materials:** Bring *Dimensional Appliqué* to class with materials for these three blocks from Lesson 7: "Crown of Ten Penny Roses" (Pattern #4), "Crown of Quilted Roses" (Pattern #5), and "Crown of Ruched Roses" (Pattern #6)

VI. A FOUR ALL-DAY OR EIGHT EVENING COURSE (EIGHT THREE-HOUR CLASSES)

Whole-Cloth Baskets Filled With Seamed-and-Turned Blooms—Begin four simple basket blocks (three from Lesson 5 in *Dimensional Appliqué* and one you choose or design yourself). Learn these fabulous techniques: The Charlotte Jane Whitehill Rose, Cannibalized Larger Prints, Sue Linker's Violets, Orchard Blossoms, Daisies, Folded-Petal Flowers, and "Bell Flowers." **Materials:** Bring *Dimensional Appliqué* to class, and materials for the first block: "Unadorned Victorian Basket of Flowers" (Pattern #12). We'll cover the basics of pattern transfer and stitching on this block. We'll go over the supplies for the subsequent blocks ("Regal Bird Amidst the Roses" and "Wilanna's Basket Garden") in class.

VII. A FOUR HALF-DAY OR FOUR EVENING COURSE (FOUR THREE-HOUR CLASSES)

Fancy Flowers Interpreted—Work three delightful Album Block patterns by Gwen LeLacheur. Follow her designs or interpret them yourselves. Learn Rick Rack Roses, Cleda's Rick Rack Blooms, Pleated Flowers, Gathered Leaves, Petals-on-a-String, Mrs. Numsen's Rose I, and Superfine Stems. **Materials:** Bring *Dimensional Appliqué* to class. Bring the materials to make "Rick Rack Roses" (Pattern #7) first. Then bring the supplies for "Baltimore Bouquet" (Pattern #21) and "I Promised You a Rose Garden" (Pattern #2)

VIII. A ONE-YEAR COURSE (TEN THREE-HOUR CLASSES)

Baltimore Basket Album—Make a basket block a month. Ten months, ten basket squares for a Baltimore Album or a Baltimore Basket Album. We'll learn lots, support each other, and be wowed with inspiration! **Materials:** The first class will be a pattern transfer and planning session. Bring *Dimensional Appliqué,* freezer paper, basic sewing kit, pencil and fabric scissors, ample yardage of your background fabric.

IX. A ONE-YEAR COURSE (TEN THREE-HOUR CLASSES)

A Wealth of Dimensional Wreaths—Open wreaths can form the matrix of an elegant Album Quilt. The theory is well explained in *Design a Baltimore Album Quilt!* Make yourself eight to ten Album cloth background blocks marked with a 4½"-radius circle (centered) on the right side of each square. We'll twine a wreath-a-month, each a study in a different kind of dimensional appliqué. We'll take our inspiration from Lesson 7 in *Dimensional Appliqué,* then lay out our garden from there! **Materials:** Bring *Dimensional Appliqué,* one circle-marked background cloth to class, a total of 30" of 1¼" bias strips for stems, and freezer paper, pencil, paper scissors, scraps of green for leaves and basic sewing kit.

X. A ONE-YEAR COURSE (TEN THREE-HOUR CLASSES)

Block-a-Month Dimensional Blooms—Album Class for the Master Album Maker. We'll choose one block from *Dimensional Appliqué* as our theme each month. You can replicate it, do a take-off on it, be inspired by it, and have the pleasure of stitching and learning ten blocks shared with like-minded friends. **Materials:** The first class will be a pattern transfer and planning session. Bring *Dimensional Appliqué,* freezer paper, basic sewing kit, pencil and fabric scissors, ample yardage of your background fabric.

ALBUM QUILT TEACHERS

Some of those who have shared their considerable talents in the *Baltimore Beauties* series, also teach locally and nationally. All of these teachers specialize both in appliqué and in those aspects of the Album Quilts represented by their needle art within the series. The following are those whose teaching I am aware of, and I pass their names on should you want to contact them. (Hometowns are noted throughout the series in the Needleartist Notes.)

Betty Alderman, Debbie Ballard, Lisa Beyers, Karen Bludorn, Wilanna Bristow, Marsha Carter, Linda Carlson, Mimi Dietrich, Zollalee Gaylor, Wendy Grande, Sue Hale, Roslyn Hay, Irene Keating, Jeana Kimball, Faye Labanaris, Gwen LeLacheur, Sue Linker, Letty Martin, Joy Nichols, Marlene Peterman, Ellen Peters, Linda Plyler, Barbara Pudiak, Gerri Rathbun, Lisa Schiller, Nadine Thompson, Annie Tuley, Alice Wilhoit. Additional teachers will be listed in the Baltimore Album Revival show catalog (April 1994).

Appendix II: Sources

If you are unable to find specialized supplies locally, they can be purchased by mail from the sources listed. Send a self-addressed, stamped envelope (SASE) for ordering information. Excellent sources appear in earlier books in this series as well.

A Token of Remembrance (Quilt #3 in the Color Section)—Jenifer Buechel, 120 Burr Street, Pittsburgh, PA 15210. Send an SASE for information on purchasing a pattern of this gem of a quilt!

Angelsea—P.O. Box 4586, Stockton, CA 95204. (209) 948-8428. A wealth of romantic ribbons (wire ribbon, iridescents, brocade/embroidered ribbons, silk filament ribbon, and more), quantity discounts, delightful! Send $3 for listing and some samples.

Sonya Lee Barrington—837 47th Avenue, San Francisco, CA 94121. (415) 221-6510. Designs tie-dyes and marbelized fabrics.

Bloomers—2975 Washington Street, San Francisco, CA 94115. (415) 563-3266. Large supply of wonderful ribbons!

Carolea's "Knitche,"—586 S. Murphy Ave., Sunnyvale, CA 94086. (408) 736-2800. Melanie Roth. Incredible notions for fancywork: scallop-edged Wiss® pinking shears, Renaissance wool for machine embroidery, Medici wool for hand embroidery.

The Caron Collection—67 Poland Street, Bridgeport, CT 08605. (203) 333-0325. "Watercolours" by Caron are choice embroidery threads, flosses, and yarns in painterly colors and color combinations.

Celtic Design Company—P.O. Box 2643, Sunnyvale, CA 94087-0643. Philomena Durcan. For information on aluminum Celtic Bars (⅛" to ½" wide) for stem-making.

Clotilde, Inc.—1909 S.W. First Avenue, Fort Lauderdale, FL 33315-2100. (1-800) 772-2891. The Quilter's favorite mail-order notions supplier! Here's where to find John James Sharps size 11, Richard Hemming's Milliner's [Straw] Needles size 10 or 11(!), Pleating pins for appliqué, Gem Tac glue, Pigma SDK permanent ink pens for drawing on fabric (including the packaged set of three ideal for detail), Metal findings for Fancy Flowers Boutique bases. Ask for Clotilde's catalog. Of particular use with *Dimensional Appliqué:* Wash-A-Way Wonder Tape (¼" wide), Clotilde's Perfect Pleater® for pleated flowers and baskets, 100%-nylon invisible sewing thread, and ThreadFuse© for use with the Perfect Pleater.

The Cotton Bale—Ann McDonald and Carol Lee Owens, 3692 The Barnyard, Carmel, CA 93923. (408) 625-2253. Good mail-order source for ribbons.

The Cotton Patch—1025 Brown Avenue, Lafayette, CA 94549. (1-800) 835-4418. Everything! Serving all of a quilter's needs by mail. The staff knows the *Baltimore Beauties* books well and understands what you are looking for, whether it be freezer paper, pens for Album blocks, the author's P & B *Baltimore Beauties* fabrics (including Classic Album Background Cloth), tie-dyes, marbelized cottons, large prints to cut up, or ribbons and notions.

Curiosity—19370 Top O' Moor Drive, Monument, CO 80132. Curiosity puts out charming patterns for appliquéd baskets, blocks, and borders. Their Petunia Basket and Poppy Basket especially appeal to me. Send SASE for information.

Debra Lund Fabrics—357 Santa Fe Drive, Denver, CO, 80223. (303) 623-2710. All cottons: tie-dyes, gradated colors, specialty fabrics, custom orders, workshops. Catalog Swatch Book, $35 refundable over the next three orders.

Decart, Inc.—Morrisville, VT, 05661, distributes Deka® paints and dyes. The Deka Oil Paintstik® is fabulous for stencil-shading fruit and flower appliqués, (Instructions in *Baltimore Beauties, Volume III.*)

Fancywork—Kathy O'Hara Light Smith, 922 McClain Road, Columbus, OH 43212-3707. (614) 486-1951. Exquisite Baltimore Album Quilt labels!

G-Street Fabrics—Mid-Pike Plaza, 11854 Rockville Pike, Rockville, MD 20852. (301) 231-8998. DMC machine embroidery thread (of the variegated green kind used in Crown of Ruched Roses; oversized rick rack, a plethora of ribbons, *crêpe de Chine,* $10 for silk samples. This is also the author's local quilt shop. She is often asked if she teaches in the Washington, D.C., area. If a class is scheduled, it will be at G-Street Fabrics, or at The Quilt Patch (Leslie Pfeiffer, proprietress), 3932 Old Lee Highway, Fairfax, VA 22030. 703-273-6937.

Howard House—1291-B Simpson Way, Escondido, CA 92029 (1-800) MARBLE. Splendid marbelized cottons!

Maret Kucera—30 South St. Albans #5, St. Paul, MN 55105, (612) 222-2483. Hand-dyed natural fibers by the yard.

Machiko Creations—P. O. Box 4313, Napa, CA 94588. (707) 224-8546. Machiko specializes in Ultrasuede brand leather materials competitively priced by the yard, in sampler packs, or in scrap bags by weight. Complete (close to 200 shades) color card: $5.

Pins & Needles — Barbara Pudiak, 282 Jefferson Ave, Fairport, NY 14450. (716) 377-2096. The pattern for the "Spring Basket Wall Quilt" pictured in the photo on page 10 is available for $8 postpaid.

Quilters' Resource, Inc.—PO Box 148850, Chicago, IL 60614. (1-800) 676-6543. A gold mine for quilt shops wanting to stock supplies for *Dimensional Appliqué!* French wire ribbon, silk thread, pins, needles, basting tape, books, and other notions. Quilters' Resource supplied the ribbon used in this book's models. For shops wishing to "kit up" Lessons 1 or 2, this is a one-stop shop!

Sew Art International—P.O. Box 550, Bountiful, UT 84011. (1-800) 231-2787. Wonderful thread source: Renaissance wool thread for the sewing machine. Sulky® forty-weight rayon (machine embroidery) thread for hand buttonholing *broderie perse* work, DMC No. 50 machine embroidery thread, 100%-cotton, including the variegated greens the author uses for embroidery leaves and rose moss.

Shades—2880 Holcomb Br. Road, #B-9, Alpharetta, GA, 30202. (1-800) 783-3933) Plentiful hand-dyed (including tie-dyed) cotton and silk fabrics.

Spoken Without A Word, A Lexicon of Selected Symbols With 24 Patterns From Classic Baltimore Album Quilts—Available from the author: Elly Sienkiewicz, 5540 30th Street, N.W., Washington, D.C. 20015. The author's first book. Original version, $19.95 postpaid. Check or Money Order to the author. Non-U.S. orders should be directed to The Cotton Patch (see page 172).

Donna Stypczynski — For information on ordering a full-size Quilters' Block Carrying Case pattern (Donna's original design), send SASE to: Hoops & Hollers, 464 Edgewood Circle, Berea, OH 44017.

Vaban/Floral—2070 Boston Drive, No. C, Atlanta, GA 30337. (1-800) 822-2606. A wealth of ribbons.

Author's Postscript

And so our page count has run out on yet another book in the *Baltimore Beauties* series. Dimensional appliqué has been especially rewarding to study. Not only are the techniques endearing, but the ethos of Baltimore clings to the air as we try each method our needlesisters share with us. The subjects themselves evoke wonder: flowers, dimension, baskets of plenty. We find ourselves looking afresh to see how a clematis is shaped, how the Lily of the Valley's rim ripples, or trying to capture the watercolor wash of a flashy, fleshy tulip.

Those ladies of Baltimore would say it was good for us, looking closely at nature. They'd commend the observant botanical detail in our quilts, applaud this pursuit of "rational pleasures." And perhaps in all our baskets and bouquets they'd see us rejoicing in the bounties of this earth, commending the beauty of this day. They might assume more fellow feeling than we yet have with them, might think we witness as openly as they, our gratitude for the earth's blessings. Or if they sensed our shyness in expressing such feelings, they might think it a bit odd, might not credit us with how far we've come. To hear it on the news, our cultural mode is gloom and doom. We struggle with contradictions. As a nation, we live better than any people on earth have ever lived. But for a moment in time (has gratitude in the land of plenty curdled into guilt?), the happy habit of publicly counting of our blessings, lags. Perhaps those ladies of bygone Baltimore call to us, saying in symbols, "Stop and smell the flowers." Reason tells us their troubles were no less than ours. With needle and thread they sang a joyful song that lifts us with its upbeat timbre. The pleasures they exalt are simple ones, available to us all: lasting pleasures, healing even. In this vein, a sign behind the desk of an otherwise homogeneous chain motel delighted me. "Practice random kindness," it urged, "Engage in senseless acts of beauty." Needleartist Jeannie Austin sent along a lovely English blessing in her correspondence. We share it here, a farewell floral wish until we meet again in *Volume III:*

"May your path be strewn with flowers,
Memories, friends, and happy hours;
May blessings come from heaven above,
To fill your life with peace and love."

About the Author

Photo by: Brian Dorfmann,
New York City

Elly's love of quilts and her initial instruction in making them came from those West Virginia relatives whom she has visited with a comforting regularity all of her life. Degrees from Wellesley College and the University of Pennsylvania led to a teaching career (history, social studies, and English) before staying at home with her three young children. Pursuing a number of entrepreneurial endeavors from home, she eventually taught quilt-making and for seven years ran a mail-order quilt supply business. Already in some demand from her first book, *Spoken Without a Word,* Elly took a brief respite from teaching and lecturing to become a tour guide for historic Washington, D.C. Refreshed and reinspired, she began to research, write, design, teach, and lecture again—a mode she's continued in happily ever since. Elly lives in our nation's capital with her husband, Stan, and their children, Donald, Alex, and Katya.

BOOKS BY ELLY SIENKIEWICZ

With the exception of her first, self-published book (see Sources), Elly's books are available from C & T Publishing, Box 1456, Lafayette, CA, 94549. Telephone: 1-800-284-1114.

Baltimore Beauties and Beyond
Studies in Classic Album Quilt Appliqué, Volume I (1989)

Baltimore Album Quilts, Historic Notes and Antique Patterns
A Pattern Companion to Baltimore Beauties and Beyond, Studies in Classic Album Quilt Appliqué, Volume I (1990)

Baltimore Beauties and Beyond
Studies in Classic Album Quilt Appliqué, Volume II (1991)

Appliqué 12 Easy Ways!
Charming Quilts, Giftable Projects, and Timeless Techniques (1991)

Design a Baltimore Album Quilt!
A Teach-Yourself Course in Sets and Borders (1992)

Dimensional Appliqué
Baskets, Blooms, and Baltimore Borders, A Pattern Companion to Baltimore Beauties and Beyond, Studies in Classic Album Quilt Appliqué, Volume II (1993)

Appliqué 12 Borders and Medallions!
Patterns From Easy to Heirloom, A Pattern Companion to Volume III of Baltimore Beauties and Beyond (1994)

Baltimore Album Revival!
Historic Quilts in the Making. The Catalog of C & T Publishing's Quilt Show and Contest (1994)

Baltimore Beauties and Beyond
Studies in Classic Album Quilt Appliqué, Volume III (1995)

Spoken Without A Word
A Lexicon of Selected Symbols With 24 Patterns from Classic Baltimore Album Quilts (self-published by the author in 1983)

Other Fine Books from C&T Publishing

An Amish Adventure, Roberta Horton

The Art of Silk Ribbon Embroidery, Judith Montano

Boston Commons Quilt, Blanche Young and Helen Young Frost

The Best From Gooseberry Hill: Patterns For Stuffed Dolls and Animals, Kathy Pace

Calico and Beyond, Roberta Horton

A Celebration of Hearts, Jean Wells and Marina Anderson

Christmas Traditions From the Heart, Margaret Peters

Crazy Quilt Handbook, Judith Montano

Crazy Quilt Odyssey, Judith Montano

Fine Feathers, Marianne Fons

Flying Geese Quilt, Blanche Young and Helen Young Frost

Friendship's Offering, Susan McKelvey

Happy Trails, Pepper Cory

Heirloom Machine Quilting, Harriet Hargrave

Imagery on Fabric, Jean Ray Laury

Irish Chain Quilt, Blanche Young and Helen Young Frost

Isometric Perspective, Katie Pasquini-Masopust

Landscapes & Illusions, Joen Wolfrom

Let's Make Waves, Marianne Fons and Liz Porter

The Magical Effects of Color, Joen Wolfrom

Mariner's Compass, Judy Mathieson

Mastering Machine Appliqué, Harriet Hargrave

Memorabilia Quilting, Jean Wells

New Lone Star Handbook, Blanche Young and Helen Young Frost

NSA Series: Bloomin' Creation, Jean Wells

NSA Series: Holiday Magic , Jean Wells

NSA Series: Hometown, Jean Wells

NSA Series: Hearts, Fans, Folk Art, Jean Wells

Pattern Play, Doreen Speckmann

Perfect Pineapples, Jane Hall and Dixie Haywood

Picture This, Jean Wells and Marina Anderson

Plaids and Stripes, Roberta Horton

PQME Series: Milky Way Quilt, Jean Wells

PQME Series: Nine-Patch Quilt, Jean Wells

PQME Series: Pinwheel Quilt, Jean Wells

PQME Series: Stars & Hearts Quilt, Jean Wells

Quilting Designs from Antique Quilts, Pepper Cory

Quilts, Quilts, and More Quilts! Diana McClun and Laura Nownes

Recollections, Judith Montano

Stitching Free: Easy Machine Pictures, Shirley Nilsson

Story Quilts, Mary Mashuta

Three-Dimensional Design, Katie Pasquini

A Treasury of Quilt Labels, Susan McKelvey

Trip Around the World Quilts, Blanche Young and Helen Young Frost

Visions: The Art of the Quilt, Quilt San Diego

Whimsical Animals, Miriam Gourley

Working in Miniature, Becky Schaefer

Wearable Art for Real People, Mary Mashuta

FOR MORE INFORMATION
WRITE FOR A FREE CATALOG FROM:

C & T Publishing
P.O. Box 1456
Lafayette, CA 94549
(1-800-284-1114)